W9-BWG-455

LIBRARY
97506

Copyright ©1970 by Holt, Rinehart and Winston, Inc.
All Rights Reserved
Library of Congress Catalog Card Number: 70–107670
SBN: 03-078210-4
Printed in the United States of America
9 8 7 6 5 4 3 2 1

Discipline a
Group Manageme
in Classroon

JACOB S. KOUNI[

Wayne State Universi[

SAIN[...] [CO]LLEGE LIBRARY
[...] [JER]SEY 07306

HOLT, RINEHART AND WINSTON, INC.
*New York Chicago San Francisco Atlanta
Dallas Montreal Toronto London Sydney*

Preface

The researches to be reported in this book started with an unintended management event in a college classroom. The author reprimanded a student for reading a newspaper during a lecture. Following this he became acutely aware that the behavior of the other students was markedly changed. Why were students who weren't targets of the reprimand affected by it? Do differences in the qualities of the reprimand produce different effects, if any, on nontarget students? These kinds of questions led to a series of researches about discipline in group situations.

The researches were designed to gain knowledge about group management techniques applicable to classroom situations. Can one predict from what a teacher does to how children behave?

A classroom consists of more than one child. These children, aggregates, subgroups, or groups, engage in a variety of activities. Some of these pertain to learning an academic subject. Some consist of intended relief from academic subjects: games, rest periods, recess. Some are intended nonacademic routines: taking attendance, collecting milk money, pledging allegiance to the flag. Events originating outside of the classroom sometimes intrude: fire engines roaring by, an older sibling bringing a note from a parent regarding special treatment for a younger child, an intercom message from the principal, an adult visitor (or an even more welcome researcher). Internal events may also intrude without the teacher's intent: misbehaviors of children, a child with sniffles, scratching caused by pinworms, a headache, a missing book, a broken pencil, a forgotten notebook, an argument. And there are disturbing nonevents: children not listening, not learning, not remembering directions.

This heterogeneity of persons, events, formats, and activity structures occurs over time as well as within any one period of time and space. At any one particular time in a classroom, different children may be doing different things at different parts of the room and with different objects and props. One subgroup may be reading with the teacher while others are engaging in seatwork. And the seatwork performers may also be doing different things, including nondoing.

The planned and unplanned realities of a classroom necessitate a teacher having skills that go beyond curricular planning and managing individual children. These skills pertain to *group* management—to what a teacher plans and does in a classroom that is aimed at more than one child and that affects more than one child.

An analysis of real classrooms reveals that there *are* concrete techniques of managing classrooms that relate to the amount of work involvement and misbehavior in learning situations. These skills go beyond those required to manage individual children. They are group management techniques that apply to boys as well as to girls, to emotionally disturbed children in regular classrooms as well as to nondisturbed children, and to both recitation and seatwork settings.

These techniques of managing classrooms were not invented by the author. Rather, they were uncovered or learned as a result of watching and analyzing videotapes of real classrooms and by comparing what teachers did in successful classrooms with what teachers did in less successful classrooms. Successful classrooms were defined as those having a high prevalence of work involvement and a low amount of misbehavior in learning settings.

The author did find it necessary to invent some names for the categories of management techniques that made a difference. The reader will confront such terminology as: withitness (demonstrating "eyes in back of one's head"); overlapping (attending to two issues simultaneously); smoothness and jerkiness (flip-flops, dangles, thrusts, stimulus-boundedness); momentum and slowdowns (overdwelling, overtalking, group-fragmentation); group-focus (group-alerting and accountability); anti-satiation (programming learning activities with variety and intellectual challenge).

The reader may miss cliches about "it all depends upon the child and the situation"; admonitions about "establish rapport," "make it interesting," "be enthusiastic"; preoccupations with personal attributes such as "friendliness," "patience," "love of children," and "understanding." Such desirable characteristics won't run classrooms.

The reader may even miss any expressed concern about educational objectives or philosophy of education. Even the best program requires good management techniques to get children started and moving. Your destination won't be reached if you can't get the car started and keep it moving (or stopped when necessary). And educational objectives won't be achieved if a teacher can't get children involved in the work or keep them from disturbing others.

This book elaborates the above categories of management techniques, presents the kind of evidence used to establish their degree of relevance to classroom management, and summarizes the researches that led to the major videotape study.

The first part of this book summarizes five years of research on the problem of discipline, defined as how a teacher handles misbehavior. Since the focus of the research was on group management, we studied how a teacher's method of handling the misbehavior of a student influences the *other* students who are audiences to the event but not themselves targets. We referred to this as the *ripple effect* in discipline.

We conducted experiments with variations in qualities of discipline techniques with college, high school, and elementary school students. All the experiments demonstrated that different techniques of handling a misbehaving student produced different kinds of effects upon audience students.

We also accumulated systematic descriptions of hundreds of discipline incidents in kindergartens and camps. There was a measurable ripple effect in kindergartens, especially on the first day. Moreover, different techniques of handling misbehavior produced different ripple effects. With but one exception, no ripple effects were discernible in camps.

In order to partly account for this apparent contradiction between the findings in kindergarten and camp, we sought to learn what children thought about misbehavior. We found that children's conceptions of misbehavior were affected by the milieu they were talking about. Their concepts about misbehavior differed depending upon whether they were talking about home, camp, or school. What is more, they had different perceptions of the disciplinary roles of parents, camp counselors, and teachers. An implication of these findings is that knowledge about disciplinary practices in homes or recreation settings cannot be directly applied to disciplinary practices in schools.

Our understanding of discipline and the ripple effect was further complicated by the results of questionnaires and interviews conducted with high school students. We found that the manner in which teachers handled misbehavior made no difference in how audience students reacted. It was not possible to predict any ripple effect from any quality of a disciplinary event as such. It was possible, however, to predict ripple effects from students' degree of motivation to learn the subject being taught. Students' degree of liking or disliking for the teacher also predicted their reactions to disciplinary events. What is more, the kinds of ripple effects influenced by motivation to learn were different from the kinds of ripple effects produced by liking for the teacher.

Experiments with high school students were then conducted to replicate the findings from the interviews and questionnaires. The findings from the experiments were opposite from the findings from the interviews. In the experiments, differences in disciplinary techniques produced different ripple effects while differences in degree of motivation to learn did not.

At this time our grant expired. We were left with many unanswered questions about disciplinary techniques and the ripple effect. There were also some seemingly contradictory findings. Results obtained in camp settings were different from results obtained in classroom settings.

This latter difference might be explained by noting that children's ideas about misbehavior and adults' roles in handling misbehavior are different in camp (and home) from what they are in school. But there were also contradictory findings between interview and experimental studies. These differences in findings might be attributable to differences between results obtained from subjects in experiments with controlled and closed methodology and results obtained from students in classrooms with a naturalistic and open method of investigation. The commitments of a subject in an experiment may be quite different from commitments of students in classrooms. Or, what happens in first contacts by way of first impressions may be different from what happens in an ongoing situation with a history.

The second part of the book deals with a different research project supported by a new grant. This second research was based upon videotapes of 80 elementary school classrooms. The videotapes enabled us to study disciplinary techniques as well as other aspects of classroom management. The reader will discover, as did the author, that there are different dimensions of group management that far outweigh disciplinary techniques in their power to influence the behavior of children in classrooms. What is more, these dimensions of group management relate to producing work involvement as well as to managing misbehavior.

The dimensions of classroom management emerging from the Videotape Studies were techniques relating to such issues as: programming learning related variety with intellectual challenge; managing activity movement; demonstrating knowledgeability of what was going on regarding children's behavior; attending to more than one issue simultaneously; maintaining group focus. To the author's knowledge, the correlations between teacher's styles of dealing with such issues and children's behavior are higher than those obtained in previous studies between *any* attribute or behavior of teachers and *any* kind of consequence in children.

The reader who is solely interested in these dimensions of classroom management and who is not concerned with research methodology as such may start by reading the second part. An understanding of the second part of the book is not dependent upon reading the first part.

In retrospect, the author must admit to having been lured into an insignificant issue when seeking to discover how discipline techniques influence behavior in classrooms. He must also admit to a sacrilegious thought in showing how the termination of grant monies benefited his understanding of classroom management by forcing him to ask other questions and to seek a new method to obtain answers. But, positive experimental findings can be quite seductive to a researcher. It may result in his continuing to ask similar questions and to develop further elaborations along the same major highway and with the same method of travel. But it may nevertheless be a blind alley if it prevents him from shifting his focus or checking his findings in reality. And perhaps it is not because variables in experimental findings are not true. It may simply be, in this case, that other variables are much more true.

And so the reader is asked to travel the whole route with the author, misleading findings and all. For, to quote Josh Billings, "It is better not to know so much than to know so many things that ain't so."

ACKNOWLEDGMENTS

The number of persons who helped supply the data for these researches is too great to permit specifying them by name. Hundreds of teachers and administrators were helpful in allowing classrooms to be observed, pupils to be interviewed, and pupils to be recruited for experiments. I wish to extend special thanks to Dr. Robert S. Lankton for his active help in all phases of data-gathering and to the teachers who allowed themselves and their classrooms to be videotaped, without even accepting a compensation of a day's dosage of tranquilizers. I can only hope that future teachers may be helped by the findings of these researches and that this will constitute their source of compensation.

Planning, conducting, and analyzing the results of the various studies was the effort of many persons. Paul V. Gump, A. Evangeline Norton, Wallace E. Friesen, James J. Ryan, III, and Sylvia Obradovic were project directors for various parts of the researches. I wish to express special obligations to Paul V. Gump for his extensive contributions.

The following persons are to be saluted for accomplishing the demanding job of coding: Frances Adams, Rose Ferber, Anita Hecker, Fayette Loria, Fern Mackour, and Kathryn Weimar. Edna Friedman deserves special commendation, not only for her technical excellence, but for managing to maintain order in what was often a confused scene.

The researches were made possible by grants M-1066 and MH-04221 from the National Institutes of Mental Health, United States Public Health Service.

Detroit, Michigan   J. S. K.
February 1970

Contents

Preface   *iii*

List of Tables and Appendixes   *xi*

PART I

STUDIES OF THE RIPPLE EFFECT IN DISCIPLINE

Chapter 1   The College, Kindergarten, and Camp Studies   1
Chapter 2   The High School Study and Some Classroom Experiments   22

PART II

THE VIDEOTAPE STUDIES OF DIMENSIONS OF CLASSROOM MANAGEMENT

Chapter 3   The Videotape Study: The Death of the Desist Technique Issue   54
Chapter 4   Withitness and Overlapping   74
Chapter 5   Movement Management: Smoothness and Momentum   92

Chapter 6   Maintaining Group Focus: Group Alerting,
                      Accountability, and Format   109
Chapter 7   Programming To Avoid Satiation   125
Chapter 8   Concluding Comments   140

References   146

Appendixes   149

List of Tables
and Appendixes

Table 1   Means of Students' Ratings of Instructor before and
           after Witnessing a Supporting and Threatening De-
           sist Technique   5
Table 2   The Relationships between Desist Qualities and Audi-
           ence Students' Reactions   29
Table 3   Product Moment Correlations between Students' Rat-
           ings of Teachers and Students' Degree of Liking for
           Teacher and Degree of Motivation To Learn the
           Subject   42

Appendix 1.1   Distribution of Audience Reactions in Kindergar-
               ten to Incidents of Low and High Desist
               Clarity   149
Appendix 1.2   Distribution of Audience Reactions in Kindergar-
               ten to Desist Incidents When Their Pre-
               Desist Orientations Were Deviant, Deviancy
               Related, or Deviancy Free   149
Appendix 1.3   Differences between the Content of Misconducts
               and Consequences for Home, School, and
               Camp Milieus   150
Appendix 1.4   Differences between the Dimensions of Miscon-
               ducts and Consequences for Home, School,
               and Camp Milieus   151
Appendix 2.1   High School Interview Schedule   152–159
Appendix 2.2   The Frequency with Which Students Use the
               Following Bases When Evaluating Teachers'
               Methods of Handling Misbehavior   160

Appendix 2.3   Frequency and Percent of Reasons Attributed to Teachers for Interfering with the Deviancy   161

Appendix 2.4   Frequency and Percent of Reasons Attributed to Teachers for Managing the Deviancy in the Manner Reported   162

Appendix 2.5   Differences between Students' Reactions to Desist Events in Classes with High and Low Motivation To Learn   163–164

Appendix 2.6   Differences between High Motivation ($N=125$) and Low Motivation Classes Determined Separately for Low Motivation Plus Teacher Liked Classes ($N = 68$) and Low Motivation Plus Teacher Disliked Classes ($N = 57$)   165

Appendix 2.7   Percentage of Students Mentioning a Teacher Attribute for High Motivation and Low Motivation Classes and for High Liked and Low Liked Teachers   166–167

Appendix 3.1   A Comparison of Attitudes toward School Misconducts Held by Children with Punitive and Nonpunitive First Grade Teachers   168

Appendix 4.1   Correlations between Teacher Style and Children's Behavior in Recitation and Seatwork Settings   169

Appendix 4.2   Intercorrelations among Teacher Style Measures   170

Appendix 4.3   Correlations and First Order Partial Correlations between Teacher Style and Work Involvement in Recitation Settings   171

Appendix 4.4   Correlations and First Order Partial Correlations between Teacher Style and Freedom from Deviancy in Recitation Settings   172

Appendix 4.5   Correlations and First Order Partial Correlations between Teacher Style and Work Involvement in Seatwork Settings   173

Appendix 4.6   Correlations and First Order Partial Correlations between Teacher Style· and Freedom from Deviancy in Seatwork Settings   174

PART I:
STUDIES OF THE RIPPLE EFFECT IN DISCIPLINE

1

THE COLLEGE,
KINDERGARTEN,
AND CAMP STUDIES

THE ACCIDENT

This series of researches started with an unintended event in my class. I was teaching a course in Mental Hygiene, devoted to understanding the psychodynamics of human behavior and intended to develop an "understanding," diagnostic attitude toward people. While lecturing, I glanced around the room and noticed a student in the back row intently reading a newspaper that he was holding completely unfolded in front of himself. Contrary to what I advocated in the course, I angrily reprimanded him without diagnosis or understanding. (I failed to administer psychological tests, to invite him for a counseling session, to interview his parents, or to study his community.)

The reprimand succeeded. He stopped reading the newspaper, or at least did not hold it completely unfolded in midair. But, the major observable impact seemed to be upon *other* members of the class. Side glances to others ceased, whispers stopped, eyes went from windows or the instructor to notebooks on the desks. The silence was heavy, as if the students were closing out the classroom and escaping to the safety of a notebook. I believe that if I had sneezed they would have written the sound in their notes.

The reprimand was not part of my lesson plan for the day, and the response of the students was quite unexpected. *They* were not reading newspapers during the lecture and *they* were not targets of the reprimand. Why were they seemingly so affected by an action of the instructor that wasn't even directed at them?

This event led to a series of studies by Dr. Paul Gump, Dr. James Ryan, and myself. (10) We started some research on what we later called the ripple effect: how a teacher's method of handling the misbehavior of one child influences *other* children who are audiences to the event but not themselves targets.

Henceforth, the term *desist* will be used to designate a teacher's doing something to stop a misbehavior. The term *ripple effect* will refer to the effect of this desist event upon other members of the classroom.

Do desists have a ripple effect? If so, what kinds of ripple effects result from a desist event? Do desists influence attitudes toward the teacher (strictness, fairness, "means business,")? Do they affect attitudes toward the deviant student or toward the deviancy? Does a desist "serve as an example" and restrain misbehavior in others? Does a desist cause other students to behave better or to pay more attention to the work at hand? Does a desist increase the tendency of others to misbehave? (It is conceivable that a teacher who says: "Jim, get away from that window and stop looking at those pretty girls in bikinis!" will stimulate other students to get out of their seats and look out the window or to draw pictures of girls on their arithmetic papers.)

In addition to the problem of designating kinds of ripple effects, there is the problem of classifying the kinds of desists. Along what dimensions do desists vary: clarity, punitiveness, anger, firmness, disapproval-focus, task-focus, intensity, humor? Do different dimensions of desists have different ripple effects? For example, does punitiveness have an effect upon attitude towards the teacher but not upon the tendency to pay more attention to the work at hand? Does firmness influence attention to the task but not attitude towards the teacher? It is clear that the issue of the ripple effect of desists could give rise to many questions.

THE COLLEGE EXPERIMENT

The first study of the ripple effect was an experiment that utilized college students. (These are captive subjects that do not require administrative clearances and parental approvals.) Four classes of students in a college of education were used as subjects. Two classes were taught by a young instructor in Education; two classes were taught by an older professor of Educational Psychology. The instructor emitted a threatening desist in one of his classes, a supporting desist in the other. The professor did the same in his two classes. This procedure resulted in two experiments; one a near replication of the other.

The scenario for the experiment ran as follows:

1. On the second day of the class a researcher, posing as a graduate student gathering data for a dissertation, administered a questionnaire to each class. These anonymous questionnaires were designed to measure students' attitudes about their instructors (this was presented as part of a social-psychological research on "first impressions" of people); the degree of seriousness of certain classroom misbehaviors (including "coming late to class"); and causes of racial prejudice (including one theory to be advocated in a later lecture by the instructor).

2. The two instructors of each of the four classes began the third class period with a lecture which gave "his own evidence" that the single most important cause of racial prejudice was repressed hostility toward punitive parents that is displaced upon minority groups.

3. A male student-stooge, previously informed about the experiment, arrived late to class and toward the end of the lectures on racial and ethnic group prejudices.

4. The instructors directed a threatening desist at the late-comer in one class and a supporting desist in the other. Both desists stated that coming late interfered with the instructors presentation and should cease. The supporting desist went on to offer the late-comer help in acquiring the lecture material he had missed. The threatening desist stated coldly that "this cannot help but affect my evaluation of you and your grade."

5. A few minutes after this event, and after the instructors finished the lecture, the "graduate student" came into the class and asked permission to readminister the questionnaire for the purpose of "establishing reliability of his measures." This was granted by the instructors, and the students complied with the request.

6. After collecting the second questionnaire, the "graduate student" explained that the desist had been contrived. He adminis-

tered a third questionnaire to determine how real the desist event seemed to the students at the time it occurred and how they felt about it.

Before arriving at definitive conclusions about the comparative effects of supporting and threatening desists one must ask whether the experimental manipulation "took." Was there a difference in how the students perceived these desists? An examination of the third questionnaire did reveal that the students saw these two different experimental treatments as different. The students rated the intended helpfulness of the instructor emitting the supporting desist as much greater than that of the instructor using the threatening desist. These differences were significant at well beyond the .001 level in both the instructor's and professor's classes.

The ripple effect may be measured by noting whether changes, beyond those attributable to chance, occur between the attitudes expressed prior to the desist and those expressed after the desist. The direction and magnitude of these changes are presented in Table 1.[1]

One may conclude that there are changes in certain attitudes that are more than chance changes. Two general conclusions are justified: (1) that students who are not themselves targets of a desist *are* affected by it; and (2) that there is a difference between the effects of a supporting desist and a threatening desist.

The next question has to do with the kinds of attitudes that are affected by desists. Students' attitudes toward the seriousness of coming late to class were not affected, and there were no differences between students who witnessed a supporting desist and those who witnessed a threatening desist in respect to this kind of judgment.

All students shifted toward the acceptance of the instructor's position that repressed hostility toward punitive parents was a major cause of racial prejudice. Nor was there any difference between those students who witnessed a supporting desist and those who witnessed a threatening desist in this respect.

The changes produced by the two differing desists were significantly different in areas relating to the evaluation of the

---

[1] A *p*-level designates the degree to which a difference is attributable to chance. A *p* of .05 may be translated to mean that the difference obtained could be obtained by chance alone 5 times out of 100; a *p* of .001 may be translated to mean that the difference could be obtained by chance 1 time out of 1000. In psychological research, a *p* level of .05 or less is conventionally regarded as statistically significant.

TABLE 1

Means of Students' Ratings of Instructor before and after Witnessing a Supporting and Threatening Desist Technique

Experimental Group	Evaluation Proposition	p-Level of Difference between Threatening and Supporting Desist
Instructor Threat	Instructor's competence	
Support	⎯⎯⎯→	.01
Professor Threat	→	
Support	┬⎯→	
	→	.60
Instructor Threat	Instructor's likeability	
Support	⎯⎯⎯→	.03
	→	
Professor Threat	⎯⎯→	
Support	←⎯	.06
Instructor Threat	Freedom to communicate	
Support	about self to instructor	.03
	⎯⎯⎯⎯⎯→	
Professor Threat	⎯⎯→	
Support	⎯⎯→	
	⎯⎯→	.42
Instructor Threat	Instructor's	
Support	nonauthoritarianism	.001
	⎯⎯→	
Professor Threat	⎯⎯→	
Support	⎯⎯⎯→	
	→	.01
Instructor Threat	Instructor's fairness	
Support	⎯⎯→	.01
	←	
Professor Threat		
Support	⎯⎯⎯→	
	←	.01

Points along the scale	(24) Definitely true	(18) Probably true	(12) Not sure, Don't know	(6) Probably not true	(0) Definitely not true

instructor and in the reported amount of felt classroom tension and discomfort.

Students who witnessed the threatening desist felt that the class was less relaxed than did students who witnessed the supporting desist.

The threatening desists, for both the instructor and the professor, resulted in significantly lowered judgments regarding their helpfulness, likeability, freedom from authoritarianism, and fairness.

It would seem, then, that differences in the effect of certain qualities of desists are more marked in some issues than in others; that the prestige and role of the emitter of the desist makes some difference; and that some norms of classroom behavior (seriousness of coming late) are so well established in colleges as to be resistant to change by an instructor's stand on the issue. The success of influence attempts of instructors that are directly related to course content (causes of prejudice) do not seem to be differentially affected by a single example of their desist technique.

However, before we form definite conclusions, let us look at the results of the post-experimental questionnaire which was designed to ascertain how the students felt about the experiment.

Although 97 percent of the students reported that they did *not* perceive that the event was contrived, they *did* report that they were surprised that a college instructor would take time out to reprimand a student for coming late, even though they rated coming late to class as a serious misbehavior. Moreover, most of the students in *all* classes reported that the use of *any* desist was *not* typical of the instructor. Classes witnessing the threatening desist described the desist as *more* atypical of the instructor than classes witnessing the supporting desist.

These reactions of surprise and perceptions of atypicality should not be ignored. Comments on the post-experiment questionnaire were in the nature of: "I felt he must have had an argument with his wife that day," or "He probably got caught in a traffic jam." (These events are evidently less unexpected than instructors reprimanding late-comers.)

What seems to be a classical experiment with controlled variables (before and after measurements, differences in treatments, similar subjects and activities, same teacher emitting the two different desists) may not be quite as pure as we thought. What is the impact of experienced surprise and perceived atypicality upon the results? Are we really studying the ripple effect of desist techniques? Or are we studying the effect of surprise and of conjectured traffic jams and arguments with wives?

From the viewpoint of research strategy these seemingly incidental by-products of the experiments might be more significant than the experimental variables. These findings point to the advisability of using teacher style variables that are within student expectations and that have some ecological prevalence.

The next study took us to real classrooms with actual teachers.

THE KINDERGARTEN STUDY

Our next step was to explore natural situations in order to ascertain the kinds of desists actually used by teachers, and pupils' reactions to these. Beginning kindergartens were selected for the first field study for several reasons:

1. Children do misbehave in kindergartens and teachers do correct them for misbehavior. Desists are, therefore, ecologically prevalent and are not unexpected.
2. Children in this group would have had little direct experience with teachers, thus permitting a study of the impact of desists relatively uninfluenced by previous relationships with teachers.
3. Special subgroup formations, which might affect the reactions of pupils in unknown ways, would be relatively absent.

Fifty-one university students were trained to obtain specimen records of desist incidents in kindergartens. These descriptive records of behavior focused upon the misbehaving child, the teacher's method of correcting his misbehavior, and the overt behavior of a child who was a witness to this desist event. Training, which occurred at five sessions over a ten-day period, included: lectures, discussions, observations and recording of role-playing sessions, mimeographed explanations and self-interrogation sheets, and practice recording in real classroom situations.

Twenty-six kindergartens in twenty schools were selected for obtaining observations. These represented the full range of socio-economic and ethnic neighborhoods in Detroit, Mich. All observations were made during the first four days of beginning kindergarten.

The job of the observer was to place himself inconspicuously in the kindergarten room and watch for an occasion in which the teacher directed a desist at a misbehaving child. The observer recorded: (1) what the deviant child and the audience pupil were doing *immediately* before the teacher intervened; (2) the full content and manner of the desist and the deviant's immediate reaction; and (3) a two-minute record of the behavior of the child nearest the deviant who was aware of the desist and who was *not* himself a target of the desist.

The observers watched carefully during the event, taking only those notes that would aid their immediate recall. Immediately after the event, they stopped observing and devoted themselves to describing the event they just observed in detail as complete as possible. After completing the writing, they readied themselves for the next desist incident.

A total of 406 incidents was employed in the data analysis. (The incidents of three out of the fifty-one observers were eliminated as inadequate for our purposes due to incompleteness or to the presence of interpretations rather than descriptions. We did not want the observer to note that the child "manifested hostility." Rather, we instructed them to write: "Johnny turned around and punched Jim on the shoulder.")

Codes were developed which provided measures for the qualities of the desist, the orientation of the audience child immediately prior to the incident, and the impact of the incident upon him.

THE INFLUENCE OF DESIST QUALITIES UPON THE RIPPLE EFFECT

A study of the desists showed that they could be scored along three major dimensions: clarity, firmness, and roughness.

Clarity refers to how much information the teacher provided in her desist. A simple "stop that," no matter how emphatically uttered, has little clarity. Nothing is specified about who the deviant is, what he did that was wrong, what he should do to correct it, or why he shouldn't do it. Clarity is added by specifying the deviant and/or the deviancy ("Billy, you are not to push in line"); by providing a way of stopping the deviancy ("Turn around and look at the blackboard with us"); by specifying a reason or group standard ("In kindergarten we ask for things. We don't grab").

Firmness refers to the degree to which the teacher packs an "I-mean-it" and a "right now!" quality into the desist. If a teacher is explaining traffic lights to a group, casually says "stop it" to a misbehaving child, and immediately resumes explaining the traffic lights, the desist possesses little firmness. Firmness is added if she has a "follow-through" and looks at the deviant until he stops; if she walks toward the child during the desist; if she speaks emphatically; if she touches or "guides" the child to the proper behavior; and the like.

Roughness refers to desists in which the teacher expresses anger or exasperation. These consist of desists containing angry looks or remarks, threatened or actual punishments, or physical pressure beyond firmness. (No examples of harsh physical treatments— shaking or spanking—were reported by the observers.)

It is also necessary to categorize the kinds of ripple effects, including "no effects." How does the audience child behave during and after the desist directed at another child?

The kinds of overt ripple effects scored were : *no reaction*—the audience child shows no behavior which the coder can interpret as related to the desist incident—if the child was drawing he simply continued his drawing; *behavior disruption*—the child shows anxiety or apprehension, confusion, increased restlessness, decreased involvement in the legitimate ongoing activity; *increased conformance*—the child's behavior was more conforming than it was previous to the desist—he stopped misbehavior of his own, paid closer attention to the lesson, stood or sat even "straighter;" *increased nonconformance*—in this case the audience child engages in a misbehavior of his own following the desist event. (For example : the teacher was explaining traffic lights to the children. John, who was sitting about two feet behind the circle, was holding one arm around Mary's waist and stroking her hair with the other. The teacher looked at them, saying: "John, come join the circle and sit here and listen while I tell you about traffic lights." John left Mary and joined the circle. Barry, who was watching John and Mary, got up from the circle, sat down next to Mary, and started to put his arm around her waist. We labeled this incident: "You can't stop the libido."); *ambivalence*—this was coded when the child showed increased conformance in one act and increased nonconformance in another act following the desist.

Having categorized properties of the desists as well as types of ripple effects we can now see whether there are ripple effects and whether different ripple effects are produced by desists that differ in their degree of clarity, firmness, and roughness.

The *clarity* of a desist did affect the ripple effect. The major effect of the clarity of a desist was to produce more conformity and less nonconformity. (See Appendix 1.1.) Children who witnessed a teacher desist another child's misbehavior in a manner that was clear, tended to conform more and misbehave less immediately following this incident than did children who witnessed a teacher emit a desist that was not clear.

The *firmness* of a desist also influenced the ripple effect. Children who witnessed a teacher utilize a firm desist tended to behave better and misbehave less than did children who witnessed a desist that was not firm. The overall impact made by clarity, however, was greater than the impact made by firmness. For example, the ratio of conformity to "no reaction" was greater for desists with clarity than for desists with firmness.

The ripple effects produced by *roughness* differed from the ripple effects produced by either clarity or firmness. Roughness produced *no* differences in the prevalence of conformance or nonconformance. Children who witnessed a teacher desist another child with anger or punitiveness did not conform more nor misbehave less than those witnessing a teacher desist another without anger or punitiveness.

Rough desist techniques did influence the proportion of "no reaction" compared to "behavior disruption" effects. The impact of roughness (as compared to no roughness) was to produce a smaller number of no reaction effects and a larger proportion of behavior disruption effects. Roughness, then, cannot be seen as simply an intensification of firmness since it has different effects.

THE INFLUENCE OF THE AUDIENCE CHILD'S ORIENTATION UPON THE RIPPLE EFFECT

Does the orientation of the audience child influence the nature of the ripple effect? Does a child react differently to a desist event if he is busy with his work than if he is himself tinged with deviancy?

The orientations of the audience children immediately preceding the desist event were categorized as *deviancy-free* (engaged in legitimate work) or *deviancy-linked* (engaged in a misbehavior themselves or else watching the deviancy). We then compared the ripple effect for those children who were oriented toward deviancy with those who were free from deviancy at the time of the desist. (The results of this analysis are presented in Appendix 1.2.)

The orientation of the audience children did make a difference in how they reacted to a desist event. Deviancy-linked children reacted with more conformance, more nonconformance, and more ambivalence than did deviancy-free children ($p < .001$). Conformance, nonconformance, or ambivalence have the property of *direction*—they are ripple effects that are directed toward conformance, or misbehavior, or both. Ripple effects that were not related to direction (signs of negative emotions or behavior disruption) were not affected by the audience children's orientation. Whether the audience children manifested no reaction to the desist or reacted by some form of behavior disruption was not influenced by whether they were engaged in legitimate work or oriented to deviancy.

Since the audience children's orientations were so significantly related to the ripple effect it seemed possible that the effects of clarity or firmness might also depend upon whether they were deviancy-linked or deviancy-free prior to the desist event. This proved to be the case.

Clarity was significantly related to increased conformity and decreased deviancy for *both* deviancy-free and deviancy-linked children. Firmness, however, was associated with increased conformance and decreased deviancy only for deviancy-linked children but not for children who were deviancy-free. In other words, a clear desist had a salutary effect on all watching children whereas a firm desist affected only those audience children who were themselves inclined toward deviancy at the time.

THE INFLUENCE OF LENGTH OF TIME IN KINDERGARTEN

The ripple effects were tabulated separately for each of the four days. An analysis of the amount and kind of reactions to desist incidents for the four different days showed significant differences. The most significant differences were between the ripple effects on the first day and those of the following three days. There were fewer reactions on the second through fourth days than on the first day ($p < .001$). A majority (55 percent) of the children witnessing a desist on the first day of kindergarten showed some outward reaction to the incident. Only a minority (34 percent) showed some overt reaction on the subsequent three days.

There was also a difference in the *kind* of overt reaction, when one did occur, between the first day and the following three days. On the first day *more* children manifested conformance and behavior disruption and *fewer* showed nonconformance ($p < .001$). On the first day of kindergarten a child witnessing a teacher correct another for misbehaving is less inclined to misbehave and more inclined to conform or to become upset than he is upon subsequent days.

SUMMARIZING COMMENTS ABOUT THE KINDERGARTEN STUDY

There is evidence for a ripple effect in real kindergartens conducted by actual teachers and with children who perceive of themselves as children in kindergartens rather than as subjects in an experiment. The degree and kind of ripple effect is influenced by at least three variables: the length of time the child has been in attendance at school, the behavioral orientation of the child witnessing the teacher's desist, and the qualities of the desist technique.

Children witnessing a desist event show more overt reaction to the event on the first day of kindergarten than they do on following days. Moreover, on the first day, they are less inclined to misbehave themselves, more inclined to conform, and more likely to show some behavior disruption and signs of negative emotionality after witnessing a teacher correct another child for misbehavior.

The behavioral orientation of the audience child immediately preceding a desist directed at another child was another significant variable influencing his reaction to the incident. Children who were deviancy-linked (either watching misbehavior with interest or misbehaving themselves) showed more conformity, nonconformity, and a mixture of both than did deviancy-free children. They also reacted differently to firmness.

The qualities of desist techniques studied that made a difference in how audience children behaved were clarity, firmness, and roughness. Desist techniques exhibiting clarity produced more conformity and less nonconformity than did desists lacking clarity. This was true for both deviancy-linked and deviancy-free children. Desist techniques showing firmness also produced more conformity and less nonconformity than did techniques lacking firmness. However, unlike clarity, this impact was present only for those children who were themselves oriented toward deviancy at the time of the desist. Roughness did not effect conformity or nonconformity. Rough techniques, compared to techniques with no roughness, resulted in more behavior disruption and in more overt signs of emotional upset. Rough desists did not make for better behavior in the watching children—they simply upset them.

THE CAMP STUDY

Armed with the increased success expectation provided by finding relationships between desist techniques and their ripple effects, and having no classrooms to observe in summer, we proceeded to study the same phenomenon in a boys' camp. We intended to replicate the findings obtained in kindergarten as well as to extend the range of the following factors: the ages of the children, the types of activity settings, the varieties of deviancies, the kinds of desist techniques, and the general leadership styles in which these are embedded.

We conducted observations in two cabin settings: morning clean-up period and afternoon rest period. These settings were deemed suitable for our purposes because the expected behavior of the children in these settings was a matter of camp-wide policy and because we expected an appreciable number of desist events to occur—children at camp aren't overly enthusiastic about making beds, cleaning cabins, or lying quietly in bunks for an hour.

The data consisted of specimen records of leaders' and campers' behaviors. Specimen records are designed to provide complete and objective records of behavior. Two observers were placed in each cabin. One observer took specimen records of the behavior of randomly predetermined campers and the other observer took records of the leader during the same period. These records were synchronized for time so that when analyzed together, they provided a running account of both leader and camper behavior as well as camper reactions (both as targets and as audiences) to desist incidents. Four cabins were chosen among the seven- through nine-year-old campers and four among the ten- through thirteen-year-old campers.

For each of eight different cabins we gathered approximately six hours of leader behavior concurrent with camper behavior in the two settings of clean-up and rest period. These observations were spread over a two-week period of time per cabin group.

Observations were also conducted in settings that were predominately instructional, such as nature study, crafts, and first aid. These were conducted by counselors who were chosen to teach these activities. These instructors dealt with groups of campers other than their own intact cabin groups. A cabin group attended each of six instructional activities about two to four times during a camping session.

Since the data gathered in instructional settings was intended to replicate those obtained in the Kindergarten Study, it was possible to use a form which precoded most of the descriptive material used in the Kindergarten Study. The precoded material included: the audience child's orientation immediately preceding the desist (deviancy-free versus deviancy-linked); the desist (clarity, firmness, roughness); and the behavior of the child for two minutes (no reaction, conformity, nonconformity, behavior disruption, and ambivalence).

RESULTS CONCERNING DESIST EFFECTS

The major ripple effect, in both cabin and instructional activities, was "no effect." The study in instructional settings was terminated after two weeks because none of the six observers (contrary to their expectations and wishes) found a sufficient number of observable ripple effects (even to the extent of "attention to the desist beyond minimal awareness") to warrant continuing this part of the study.

Nor (unlike the Kindergarten Study) was there any relationship between the degree of clarity, roughness, or firmness of the desist and the kind of ripple effect. The only quality of a desist that made any difference was one that contained high attraction novelty (talk about a watermelon party or a camp carnival) and this produced "attention above the minimum required for awareness" but had *no* impact upon conformity, nonconformity, or behavior disruption.

At this point, we were forced to conclude that the ripple effect of leader desist techniques, as judged by overt campers' reactions, was ecologically infrequent, and perhaps unimportant. We also were getting the *impression* that other dimensions of group management far overshadowed desist style in influencing campers' overt behavior. Our impression was that "good" leaders produced conformity (cleaning up or resting) regardless of how they desisted a deviancy and the "poor" counselors did not. The leadership styles around which we designated "good" and "poor" counselors at this time were quite impressionistic and were based upon simple categories rather than upon behavior measurements. These categories of leadership style included such judgments as excessive punitiveness, excessive psychological and physical absenteeism, and excessive floundering and purposelessness.

The only reservation we would put on the conclusion that ripple effects of desists were unimportant in the camp settings has to do with the matter of unobservable, covert effects of leader desist techniques. Our observations were limited to observable behavior. Might desist styles influence campers in ways that were not apparent in their overt behavior?

THE SUPEREGO STUDY

In an effort to ascertain some covert effects of the children's camp experience, we interviewed, individually, all campers from the cabins studied on the last day of their camp stay. Of special concern here is the section of the interview having to do with their attitudes toward misconduct. We labeled this the Superego Study (more for the purpose of brevity than precision).

Each child was asked to: "Think about the camp. What is the worst thing a kid could do at camp?" After the reply, the child was asked: "Why is that so bad?" He was then asked for the next worst thing a kid could do at camp as well as for the reason for its being so bad. These questions were then asked about home and about school.

We deliberately chose an open-ended method to study children's attitudes toward misconduct. We wanted to learn about their attitudes and perceptions and not what they thought about what we thought. Consequently we did not present them with any adult-structured scales or measuring devices. For example, if we had asked them whether "murdering someone" was worse than "talking when another child was reading" they undoubtedly would have rated murder as a more serious offense than talking (and might even have thought we were stupid for asking such a silly question). Nevertheless, they didn't spontaneously talk about murdering. Rather, they talked about much more trivial matters like breaking lamps, making noise in halls, hitting the other kids, having pillow fights during rest period, and the like. The misconducts they talked about, then, are most likely reflections of their concerns, their experiences, their unresolved issues, their desires or impulses, their preoccupations, and what they perceived as salient and significant about misconduct in the milieu they were talking about.

What do the children talk about? What can we learn from what they say? Do they carry within themselves a situation-free concept of misbehavior that is independent of the milieu they are in, or do their preoccupations about misbehavior relate to the milieu as well?

When we tried to listen to what they had to say about misbehavior we heard many different things. The categorizations of their responses are summarized in Appendix 1.3 and Appendix 1.4. Some of the categories refer to the contents of their responses such as: the kind of misconducts, who or what is harmed, the kind of harm or suffering caused, who or what punishes the perpetrator, and the kind of punishment it is. Other categories refer to certain qualities or dimensions that cut across all kinds of misconducts and consequences such as: the amount of destructiveness, the degree of seriousness, the degree of realism, the intention of the perpetrator.

CONTRAST BETWEEN CAMP AND SCHOOL MISCONDUCTS

Of special significance for research on the management of misbehavior are the findings comparing the children's responses to camp and school. An analysis of the responses revealed many differences between the kinds and qualities of the misconduct concerns expressed by the children for camp and school.

The misconducts talked about in camp are more trivial than those discussed about school, are morally more inconsequential, and are less likely to actually happen in camp than are the misconducts discussed about school likely to happen in school.

In spite of the inconsequentiality and triviality of the camp misconducts, the amount of destructiveness going along with these misconducts is much greater in camp than in school. (For example: "Play in the storage bin. . . . You could push a kid off and there could be a sharp rock down there, and he could hit his head against it, and bust open his head and he would bleed and his brains would fall out and he'd die.") This greater aggressivity is more apparent when directed against persons than when directed against objects.

Another major difference between children's misconduct concerns in camp and school relates to the role of self in misconduct. In school, the child's misconducts are intentional ("talk during a lesson") while in camp they are premeditated ("wait until the counselor leaves, then clobber Jimmy"). That is, the child admits and accepts his part in wrongdoing in school but does not plan this misconduct nor intend harmful consequences. In camp, the child tends to actually plan his misconducts. Moreover, the child sees himself as paying for his misconducts in school—he suffers some retribution. In camp, others suffer but the perpetrator does not. In addition, the child in camp is preoccupied with misconducts that are ego alien and for which he expresses abhorrence. In school, the child concerns himself about misconducts that are more ego acceptable—which are neither particularly fascinating or seductive for him nor particularly repulsive.

In summary, in camp as compared to school, the child concerns himself with trivial and morally inconsequential misconducts, colors them with a high degree of unlikely aggression and destructiveness to other persons, selects misdeeds for which he has abhorrence and yet which require planning or "malice and forethought," and evades accepting his responsibility or suffering the consequences.

We conducted the Camp Study in order to replicate the findings from the Kindergarten Study. In kindergarten, we found a ripple effect as well as a relationship between some qualities of teachers' desist techniques and the kind and degree of ripple effect. In camp we found neither a significant number of ripple effects nor any relationships between a counselor's techniques of desisting and the kind of ripple effect when one did occur.

The question arises as to why the findings in camp are different from those in kindergartens. Without enumerating possible explanations for these differences, it suffices, at this point, to merely accentuate the fact that there are differences between camp and school. And without enumerating differences in the ecologies of the two milieus we may point out that there are consequential differences in respect to the crucial variable being investigated, namely children's misconduct and its handling by the central adult. Not only do children have different conceptions about misconduct in camp from those in school but they also see the role of the camp counselor in this respect as different from the role of the teacher.

CONTRASTS BETWEEN HOME AND SCHOOL IN CHILDREN'S CONCEPTIONS OF MISCONDUCT

There are also differences between home and school in terms of how children perceive misconducts and how they perceive parents' and teachers' roles as both objects of, and retributors for, children's misconduct. And, since so much of our ideology about discipline and about adult-child relationships derives from studies of parent-child relationships (frequently extrapolated without modification to teacher-child relationships) we thought it worthwhile to further study children's conceptions of home and school misconduct.

In order to study differences between home and school more intensively and to obtain a greater number of younger children than were available in camp, we interviewed 227 children from six urban schools representing a range of socio-economic backgrounds. Boys ($N=113$) and girls ($N=114$) were interviewed during their first semester in the first grade and again two years later. The interviews utilized Superego questions for home and school milieus only.

There were consistent differences between school and home in the kinds of misconducts talked about. *Breaking objects* was predominantly a home misconduct for both boys and girls and for both first and third grades ($p < .01$). *Nonconformance* with the central adult was much greater in home than in school ($p < .01$ for the first grade and $< .08$ for the third grade). Direct disobedience or defiance of teachers was a rarely reported misconduct, but such affronts to parents were reasonably frequent.

Assaults on children were reported more frequently for school than for home. Boys had more assaults on other children in school in both first and third grades ($p < .01$); girls showed this same school-home contrast in the third grade ($p < .02$). In the first grade, the girls showed a greater preoccupation with *rule violations* ("Go visit a friend without asking first." "Talk when you're supposed to study.") in school than in home ($p < .001$). This greater concern with rule violations by girls for school derived from their more frequent reporting of *talking* as a misconduct. Talking was reported by one girl in four in the first grade; by one of eight in the third grade. Boys did not discuss talking as much as did girls. (The reader is free to form his own conclusions about the generality of this finding to men and women.)

Another difference between home and school had to do with the relative extent of simple *inconvenient* acts reported as misconducts. Inconvenient acts are those which are disturbing but are without direct harm to the perpetrator or to others and which do not violate any important moral taboo. The flavor of this type of misconduct can be best conveyed by the following examples: "run in the halls," "throw paper," "run around and make noise," "play around at bedtime." Such inconvenient misconducts were mentioned more frequently for school than for home ($p < .001$ in the first grade and $p < .01$ in the third grade).

A child may explain that a misconduct is bad because it results in some harm to the perpetrator, it harms other persons, or it is just wrong ("It's bad because it's bad," or "it's bad because it's not nice," or "because it's wrong"). The latter were called *reflexive justifications*. Reflexive justifications as reasons for regarding a misconduct as bad were given for more school misconducts than for home misconducts by both boys and girls ($p < .01$ for first grade and $p < .05$ for the third grade). Inspection of the data showed that the higher proportion of reflexive justifications at school was associated with their greater use in conjunction with rule violations which have greater prevalence in reports about school misconducts. This difference in the use of reflexive justifications may be a consequence of reality differences between home and school and may also reflect these children's naïve trust in school, resulting in their saying that something is bad simply "because they say so."

Two other consistent contrasts had to do with the role of the central adult. Only parents were seen as suffering as a result of a child's misconducts. Parents worried or had to pay repair bills. Teachers almost never suffered ($p < .001$).

Just as the milieu influenced whether or not the central adult suffered, it also influenced the type of punishment this central adult administered. In the first grade, parents were reported as using corporal punishment in 64 percent of their punishments, teachers 22 percent ($p < .001$). By the third grade, corporal punishment by adults was markedly reduced, but home tended to maintain the greater proportion. This difference may or may not reflect the actual amount of corporal punishment used by parents or teachers. It does mean that children perceived it that way, or were thus concerned about it, or saw it as the legitimate function of parents and teachers.

This second Superego Study shows considerable agreement with the Camp Study in spite of differences in age level, the addition of girls to the sample, and the order and setting in which the questions were asked.

In summary, both studies showed, among others, the following differences between home and school as regards the type of children's misconduct concerns: school contained more misconducts in which other children are the objects of attack, and had more rule violations and milieu inconvenient misconducts; home misconducts were more weighted toward breaking of objects, fire play, and nonconformance with adults. As regards the explanations of why misconducts were bad: school explanations emphasized reflexive justifications, children suffering, and noncorporal punishment; home explanations emphasized adult suffering and corporal punishment.

There are, then, consistent differences in children's conceptions of misconduct depending upon whether they are talking about home, school, or camp. Of special significance for this research are the differences in children's perceptions of the role of the central person in these situations insofar as they are objects, sufferers, or retributors in misconduct issues. And, since so many opinions about discipline are derived from studies of parent-child relationships simply generalized to teacher-child relationships, one is justified in being cautious about engaging in such extrapolations.

And so our Camp Study, and the tangential Superego Interview Study, impelled our returning to school milieus to study the ripple effect.

2
THE HIGH SCHOOL STUDY
AND SOME CLASSROOM
EXPERIMENTS

The next study was a further attempt to see what could be learned about how students reacted to an incident in which a teacher desisted another student for some classroom misconduct. Since both the Kindergarten and Camp Studies concentrated upon overt behavior as described by an outside observer, we decided to probe the issue further by studying how audience students themselves saw the issue and reacted to it.

THE HIGH SCHOOL INTERVIEW

In order to secure this information, interviews were conducted with students who were just entering high school. The students, randomly selected, included sixty-three boys and sixty-two girls. They were interviewed between the fourth and tenth days of their attendance at the school and again three months later. One high school was located in a predominantly lower-class neighborhood, one in a lower-middle-class area, and the third in a middle-middle-class nieghborhood.

This entire interview schedule was conducted twice for each student—once for the academic class with the student's highest degree of motivation to learn and again (during the same interview session) for the class with the student's lowest degree of motivation to learn. The interview schedule is presented in Appendix 2.1.

THE KINDS OF MISBEHAVIORS AND DESISTS

In order to provide some reality to the reader, we will present some descriptive findings about the misbehaviors and the desist styles before discussing statistical relationships between them. What kinds of misbehaviors occurred and what steps did teachers take to stop them?

Most of the misbehaviors discussed by the students fell into the following categories: talking, 30 percent; noise, laughter, and loud talking, 25.2 percent; nontask orientation (engaging in some type of nontask activity when an official task involvement was the legal activity), 17.2 percent; gum chewing, 6.8 percent. The rest of the deviancies consisted of arriving late, failure to bring homework or appropriate props (pencils, books), and moving around the room at a time or place when such movement was illegal.

The descriptions of the deviancies were categorized to determine the degree to which the deviancies interrupted or "pushed into" the official activity of the class at the time. Most of the deviancies (46 percent) were coded as having low intrusion. Here, the extent of inroad into the classroom's general activity is relatively minor, but there is no doubt that the deviancy is present. (An example: "Two boys behind me were talking"). Thirty-two percent of the reported deviancies were rated as average (18 percent) or as high (14 percent) in intrusiveness. These were deviancies that were both clearly perceptible and were significantly distracting. Examples are: "This boy was making noise with his feet;" "A boy *kept* leaving his seat and going over to talk to a girl." A "trivial" rating was given to 16.4 percent of the deviancies, and an "extreme" rating was given to 5.6 percent. The latter was given to deviancies that were clearly and excessively distracting, such as: "This boy in back of the room was singing to himself;" ". . . he started stamping his feet up and down and drumming on his desk with his hands."

---

[1]A more complete presentation of the codes and results is available in the dissertation of Leon T. Ofchus (13).

The students' verbatim accounts of the desist techniques made it possible to discern three major foci of the teachers' efforts: the teacher could punish; the teacher could simply order the student to stop the misbehavior—a desist; the teacher could move the deviant into some form of legal activity—an induction. Over one half of the described events (54 percent) contained some form of punishment. Noteworthy because of its infrequent use (in 8.4 percent of the cases) was "induction"—moving the deviant into some kind of legal activity as a means of stopping misbehavior.

When punishment was used or threatened, what kind of harm befell the deviant? When punishment was used it involved sending to the counselor (16.4 percent), the imposition of additional work or time (12 percent), or sending the deviant to another section of the room (8.4 percent). Physical contact occurred in but two of 250 desists. The degree of harm threatened or done to the deviant was also rated. How much was the deviant made to suffer, squirm, or feel psychological hurt? In 43.2 percent of the cases the deviant either was administered no harm (40 percent) or trivial harm (3.2 percent). A trivial harm consisted of: "Will you please be quiet?" or a simple "looked at him and smiled slightly." Sharp or moderate harm was administered or threatened in 51.2 percent of the cases. These would cause a deviant to feel uneasy or embarrassed ("Stop pestering the girls, or get out into the hall") or a substantial pain of sorts ("You lose five points off your grade for chewing gum," "If you can't keep quiet, you can go to your counselor."). Extreme harm (here defined as sarcasm, ridicule, threatened failure in course) was present in 5.6 percent of the events.

The dimension of clarity was rarely applicable when describing the teachers' desist styles. In 92 percent of the cases, the teacher gave no reason for why the misbehavior was bad; in 95.6 percent of the cases, the teacher gave no specifications about any kind of group standards; and the teacher gave specific elaborations of reasons for desisting in only 6 percent of the desist events. One may say that the vast majority of the desists contained little information beyond "stop it" and "I'll punish you in some way."

How did students who were audience to these events react to them? We are interested here in those effects spontaneously suggested by the students in response to the open-ended questions. Presumably, responses to open-ended questions reveal what is salient to the student himself, and around what kinds of ways he sees himself as reacting to the desist event.

The most frequently mentioned consequence of the desist event was some felt emotion. Some kind of affect was spontaneously reported by 15.2 percent of the students. About half of these feelings (7.2 percent) were pleasant affects: "I was glad that he got it;" "Happy it came out that way because he is a friend of mine." The remainder were either unpleasant affects ("I felt sad because he was kicked out."), or expressions of fear ("I was scared," "She really scared me, she was so mad."), or anger at either the teacher or the deviant.

The issue of behavior conformity was brought up by 11.6 percent of the students. An increased tendency to behave better, or resolve to behave better, was stated by 11.2 percent of the students in such spontaneous responses as: "When she stopped foolin' around, it was easier for us to behave;" "I decided to keep quiet so I could hear the instructions." A tendency toward less conformity was mentioned by but 0.4 percent of the students. An impact upon task involvement was mentioned by 5.2 percent of the students; 4.4 percent increased or resolved to increase their task involvement and 0.8 percent decreased their task involvement. Included in the task involvement category were such comments as: "Made sure I got my work done;" "When she stopped them, the other kids paid attention."

Attitudes toward the deviant or the deviancy were mentioned as having been affected by 7.6 percent of the students. This area of impact was exemplified by such statements as: "He shouldn't have been fooling around;" "I didn't like him anyway."

Opinions about the teacher constituted another area of saliency to the students. Eight percent of these comments had to do with the perceptions of teachers as controllers of deviancy as such: "He means business;" "He's easy;" "Made me wonder if he could handle kids;" "Boy, he's hard on kids." The remainder (7.2 percent) of the comments about teachers had to do with more general teacher characteristics, such as: "She is a nice person;" "She wants kids to learn;" "She just never gives kids credit for anything."

One might summarize the descriptive findings about misbehaviors and desists, and students' reactions to these events as follows:

1. The kinds of deviancies reported were predominantly infractions of classroom rules: talking, noise and laughter, and lack of task orientation. For the most part, these possessed low intrusiveness into the class routine, were of moderate noticeability, and lacked any moral seriousness or harm to self or others.

2. Teachers were reported as handling deviancy mainly with some form of punishment or by simple orders to stop. The punishments most frequently used were sending the deviant to his counselor or imposing extra work or time. In most cases, the amount of harm administered to the deviant could be rated as moderate or none. (It should be noted that ridicule, sarcasm, or failing grades were rated as "extreme harm" on the scale of harmfulness.) In a majority of desists, the students reported the teacher as being mildly angry and as showing moderately high determination to stop the reported misbehavior.

3. Students perceived the teachers as interfering with deviancy primarily to maintain or restore a learning climate, secondarily to reaffirm and maintain classroom conventions, and lastly to express personal impulses or reduce personal discomfort. A majority of students expressed some degree of approval for the teachers' interfering with the reported misbehavior.

4. Students evaluated teachers' methods of handling misbehavior, whether favorably or unfavorably, around the issues of justice and fairness, effectiveness, and the appropriateness of the intensity of the teachers' reactions to the deviancy.

5. When asked why they thought a teacher chose the method of desisting that she used, the students attributed the following kinds of intents to the teachers, in order of their frequency of mention: to limit the severity of harm to the deviant, to express their own feelings or limit their own discomfort, and to facilitate other students' learning.

6. Fewer than half of the incidents resulted in any spontaneously reported effect upon the student audience. When an impact was reported, the impact was felt predominantly around some kind of positive or negative emotion, a limited change in student attitudes toward the teacher (mostly around the dimension of strictness), a tendency to behave better themselves immediately following a desist event, and a slight inclination to pay more attention to the official task at hand. (Except for attitudes toward a

teacher, these are the same dimensions of effect measured in the Kindergarten Study.)

RELATIONSHIPS BETWEEN DESIST QUALITIES AND THE RIPPLE EFFECT

The original purpose of this research project was to see if there was any relationship between a teacher's desist technique and the ripple effect. This line of inquiry was exemplified in the Kindergarten Study where a relationship was found between qualities of desist techniques (clarity, roughness, firmness) and the ripple effect (conformity, task involvement, and signs of emotional upset).

The qualities of the desists measured in the High School Interview were: presence of punishment, amount of harm to the deviant, clarity, firmness, anger, and presence or absence of humor. The ripple effects were: behavior conformity, attention to the task, siding with the teacher or the deviant, and emotional discomfort.

Is there any relationship between the qualities of a teacher's desists and the ripple effect? *The major effect was "no effect."* As summarized in Table 2, the predominant result for most classrooms was that differences in clarity, firmness, punishment, and humor of desists *produced no difference* in the number of students who conformed, paid attention to the task, sided with the teacher or deviant, or became upset or uncomfortable. (NS means that there is *no significant difference.*)

The only relationship that was significant for both classes (high motivation to learn and low motivation to learn) was that between a desist that contained anger and the reporting of some felt emotional discomfort. (This is consistent with the results obtained in the Kindergarten Study showing behavior disruption consequent to a teacher's having some roughness in her desist.) The presence of punishment increased student attention to the task only in classes where a student had high motivation to learn the subject. Punishment had no impact in classes where students had low motivation to learn, nor was it a significant factor when all classes were combined. A teacher's firmness increased students' inclinations to behave better but only for those students reporting about classes where they had a high motivation to learn the subject. When all classes

TABLE 2   The Relationships between Desist Qualities and Audience Students' Reactions[a]

Desist Quality	Conformity		Attention		Side with Teacher or Deviant		Emotional Discomfort	
	High Motivation To Learn	Low Motivation To Learn	High Motivation To Learn	Low Motivation To Learn	High Motivation To Learn	Low Motivation To Learn	High Motivation To Learn	Low Motivation To Learn
N	125	125	125	125	125	125	125	125
Described punishment	NS	NS	.05	NS (.80)	NS	NS	NS	NS
Described harm	NS	NS	NS	NS	NS	NS	NS	NS
Described clarity	NS	NS	NS	NS	NS	NS	NS	NS
Rated anger	NS	NS	NS	NS	NS	NS	.001	.05
Rated firmness	.01	NS (.30)	NS	NS	NS	NS	NS	NS
Rated humor	NS	NS	NS	NS	NS	NS	NS	NS

[a]NS = Difference by x^2 test above .10 level.

were combined, or in classes where students had low motivation to learn, firmness made no difference.

RELATIONSHIPS BETWEEN DEGREE OF MOTIVATION TO LEARN AND THE RIPPLE EFFECT

In addition to inquiring about how students reacted to a desist event, we also attempted to explore a general hypothesis; namely, that a student's degree of motivation to learn the subject matter influences the manner in which he reacts to a teacher desisting the misbehavior of another student in the class. In order to study this hypothesis we had each student rate his degree of motivation to learn each of his academic subjects. By comparing the reactions of the same students to a desist in their high motivation classes and their reactions to a desist in their low motivation classes one may arrive at some findings about this question. Differences could then be attributable to differences in strength and direction of motivation since the persons are the same.

The results of this comparison are presented in Appendix 2.5. These results are grouped into five categories, as follows:

Students' Behavior Reactions
Students who were witnessing a desist event in a class where they were highly motivated to learn the subjects reported that they were inclined to behave even better after the event than students in a class where they had low motivation to learn. They also tended to report a greater inclination to increase their attentiveness than did the low motivation group. However, it should be noted, that since they were already higher in attentiveness than the low motivation group, they had less probability of being able to move higher.

Students' Judgments about the Desist Event
These measures have to do with how the students judged and evaluated the desist event. The students in classes with high motivation to learn clearly evaluated the incidents in more of a pro-teacher manner than did the same students in classes where they had low motivation to learn. In their high motivation classes, students tended to express more approval of how the teacher handled the misbehavior, tended to side more with the teacher than

with the deviant, judged the teacher more frequently as handling the misbehavior with the right amount of intensity (or even as "not tough enough on him"), and rated the teacher's method of handling the misbehavior as having a greater degree of fairness.

Judgments about the Deviancy

The two groups of students did not rate the seriousness of the misbehavior any differently. However, students in high motivation classes did describe more intrusiveness qualities of the deviancies— did bring out more of those aspects of a misbehavior that interfere with other students' learning or concentration.

Perceptions of the Desist Technique

These judgments have to do specifically with the students' descriptions of how the teacher handled the misbehavior. The students in low motivation classes reported more "pure punishment" events ("sent to counselor," "took five points off grade") in the description without any desist content ("stop that noise") or induction content ("get back to work"). The students in low motivation classes also rated the teachers' degree of anger as much higher. The descriptions in the high motivation classes contained more details about what the teacher said about deviancy and why or how to stop it. These students with high motivation to learn may be said to have picked up, recalled, and reported more about the teachers' attitudes toward misbehavior and actions to remove these learning barriers.

Attributed Reasons for Teacher Desisting

When replying to the questions of why teachers interfered and why they handled the misbehavior the way they did, students with high motivation to learn gave different kinds of reasons than did the same students with low motivation to learn. The high motivation group believed that teachers interfered with misbehavior in order to maintain or restore a good learning situation, and believed that teachers handled the misbehavior in the manner they did because they wanted to minimize the damage to, and protect the feelings of, the deviant. The low motivation students were more inclined to believe that teachers did what they did to express their own feelings and reduce their own discomfort. When they did approve of a desist technique the low motivation group tended to approve on the basis of fairness; the high motivation group on the basis of its effectiveness in restoring or maintaining a learning climate.

It began to look as though the theory that the intensity of motivation to learn influences how students react to a desist event is supported. In high motivation to learn, one might theorize that there is a strong goal of learning, the teachers are perceived as a path to this goal, and misbehavior is perceived as a barrier. It follows that high motivation students will: (1) react more positively to teachers who utilize their power to remove barriers to learning; (2) judge desist events more around learning relevant dimensions; (3) be more attuned to task dimensions of desist events; and, (4) react to desist events with more task related behavior.

So far, then, it looked as though an hypothesis had been strongly supported, and with more than one kind of variable. This might well have been our conclusion had we not asked some other questions of the students which appear to complicate this picture. A look at "degree of liking for the teacher" seemed to show that this variable played a noticeable part in judgments about desist events.

RELATIONSHIPS BETWEEN DEGREE OF LIKING FOR THE TEACHER AND THE RIPPLE EFFECT

The students were asked to rate their degree of liking for the two teachers by marking on a scale from "dislike very much" to "like extremely well." These points were dichotomized into high liking and low liking. In terms of descriptive points on the scale, high liking was anything *above* "neither like nor dislike." Another independent measure of liking for the teacher was obtained from a different part of the interview where the students were asked what they would tell a friend about each of the two teachers. These open-ended responses were dichotomized into "recommend to a friend" and "not recommend to a friend." Since the recommendation-dichotomies agreed with the liking-dichotomies 98 percent of the time, one may have a high level of confidence in these dichotomies and assume that they reflect the genuine global attitude of the students about the teachers.

The results showed a high relationship between liking for the teacher (or recommending the teacher) and motivation to learn the subject. In the high motivation to learn classes, 107 students had some liking for the teachers and only eighteen were neutral toward or disliked the teachers. In the low motivation to learn classes, sixty-eight had some liking for the teachers and fifty-seven were either indifferent toward or disliked the teachers.

An analysis, identical with the one summarized in Appendix 2.5, was made comparing the reactions of students in the low motivation to learn group who liked their teacher with those who did not. The results were essentially the *same* as those obtained when high motivation to learn was compared with low motivation to learn.

Liking for a teacher and motivation to learn an academic subject, then, are highly related. Not only are these variables associated with each other, but they are also associated with students' reactions to a desist event in the same direction and approximate magnitude. As it now stands, a seemingly well-supported theory relating a student's motivation to learn to his reactions to a desist event is not so obvious nor so clearly supported. Had we not happened to ask students about how much they liked or would recommend a teacher we would have been more "certain." (Similarly, we might have been more "certain" about the findings of the College Experiment had we happened not to ask the students about what they thought of the experimental event and discovered that our clean experimental variables were contaminated by the variable of unexpectedness and surprise.)

We are now left with the problem of determining how much the ripple effects are determined by motivation to learn and how much they are influenced by liking for the teacher. The differential impacts of motivation to learn and liking for the teacher can be unraveled by an additional statistical analysis. The high motivation group (HiM), which is also high in liking for the teacher, can be compared with two groups of low motivation (LoM): one with high liking for the teacher (LoM & HiL), and one with low liking for the teacher (LoM & LoL). Differences between HiM and LoM & HiL, if obtained, could be attributed to differences in motivation to learn, since both of these groups have high liking for the teacher. If there is no difference between HiM and LoM & HiL (if differences in motivation to learn make no difference) and there *is* a difference between HiM and LoM & LoL then this difference can be attributed to differences in liking for the teacher. These comparisons are presented in Appendix 2.6.

Students' reactions pertaining to attention to the task and inclination to behave even better after a desist event show significant differences between the high motivation classes and the low motivation classes both for those low motivation classes where the teacher is liked and where she is not liked. This kind of difference is also indicated for students describing and reporting intrusiveness into learning conditions as an attribute of the misbehavior that the teacher desisted. It should be noted that these kinds of student reactions are, then, mainly a function of the students' task motivation and are apparently *not* associated with his general liking for, or recommendation of, the teachers involved.

The judgments pertaining to the teachers' behavior when desisting show significant differences between teachers who are liked and those who are not liked. Teachers who are disliked are more frequently described as exhibiting more anger, as being more punitive, and as exerting more effort to stop the misbehavior than are teachers who are liked. These differences in the perceived behavior of teachers operate independently of the students' degree of motivation to learn the subject.

With respect to the measures which represent the students' evaluations of the teachers handling of the desist event, the students who dislike the teachers evaluate them as making too much of an issue about the misbehavior, as being less fair, and they less frequently support the teacher as opposed to the deviant. These differences in evaluations are associated with liking for the teacher and not with motivation to learn.

The motivation to learn theory that was presented earlier in this chapter is apparently an oversimplification of how students react to a desist event. Liking for the teacher, though highly associated with motivation to learn, appears to relate to as many, if not more, of the responses measured than does motivation to learn. (Whether one variable relates to as many, more, or less than another variable, depends, of course, upon the number of variables an investigator chooses to measure and succeeds in so doing.) Motivation to learn is associated with attention to the official learning task and a tendency to behave "even better" after a desist event. Judgment about the desist technique and the teacher, however, varied with liking for the teacher. Liking for the teacher predicted judgments of fairness and siding with the teacher over the deviant; disliking the teacher was associated with seeing anger, punitiveness, and overreacting to the deviancy. Knowledge of both motivation to learn and liking for the teacher help predict ripple effects, but they relate to different facets: Motivation to learn predicts reactions regarding the task and behavior conformance; liking for the teacher predicts to evaluative judgments regarding teachers' behaviors in the event.

The above comparisons were made for all the desist events: 250 desists involving sixty-four different teachers and 125 different students. Do these findings hold for all types of desist events or only for certain kinds? Is the predictability of the ripple effect improved by knowing the qualities of the desist event in addition to knowing the students' motivation to learn and liking for the teacher? Up to this point in the data analysis we found that the clarity, firmness, punishment, harm, and humor did *not* predict students' reactions for either high or low motivation conditions. (The only desist quality that made a consistent difference was that of anger—which produced reported emotional discomfort, but had no impact upon conformity or attentiveness to the task.) However, it is still possible that desist qualities help predict the ripple effect if both liking for teacher and motivation to learn are also known.

A THEORY RELATING THE RIPPLE EFFECT TO DESIST QUALITIES, LIKING FOR TEACHER, AND MOTIVATION TO LEARN

In order to answer whether some combinations of motivation to learn, liking for teacher, and desist qualities would predict the ripple effect, the students were grouped in four categories: (1) high motivation to learn with high liking for the teacher; (2) high motivation to learn with low liking for the teacher; (3) low motivation to learn with low liking for the teacher; and (4) low motivation to learn with high liking for the teacher.

Two questions may be asked regarding any of the above comparisons: (1) *Within* any one group, does it make any difference whether a desist technique does or does not have a certain quality? For example, do the students in the high motivation with high liking group react any differently to a desist that contains punishment than to one that does not? Do the students in the low motivation and low liking group react any differently to a desist that contains anger than to one that does not? and so on for each group and for each quality of desists. (2) Are there differences *between* groups in how the students react to a desist technique of a certain quality? For example, do the pupils in the low motivation with high liking group react differently to a desist technique containing punishment than do the students in the low motivation with low liking group? Do the students in the high motivation with low liking group react differently to a desist technique containing anger than the students in the low motivation with low liking group?

One of the concepts that is to be used in organizing and summarizing the data is that of *commitment*. We are assuming that motivation to learn a subject and liking for the teacher are *prevailing* variables. That is, they are predispositions extending over time. When a student says that he is highly motivated to learn geometry, we assume that he is talking about more than a specific theorem that he wants to learn from between 1: 00 and 1: 15 on the particular afternoon of the interview. There may be momentary vacillations in motivation, but the *overall* motivation to learn is high and present for more than one theorem, hour, or day. Similarly, we assume that the degree of liking or recommending the teacher is an attitude lasting more than one class period and referring to some global dimensions, however nebulous the source of these might be. These relatively lasting attitudes may be called commitments or predispositions. Students in the high motivation with high liking group may be thought of as being committed in a positive direction to both the task and the teacher. Students in the low motivation with low liking group have a low commitment, if any, to the task and no commitment, or a negative commitment, to the teacher. Some students may be said to have mixed commitments.

The ripple effects will also be categorized in order to facilitate presenting the findings. The students' reactions may be categorized as follows:

1. *Task related reactions.* These are the reactions having to do with the students' orientation to the official classroom requirements at the time. Measures of these are : inclina-

tion to pay more or less attention or to behave better or worse following a desist.

2. *Teacher evaluations.* These are reactions having to do with favorable or unfavorable evaluations of the teacher's behavior in the desist event. The measures of these are: whether the teacher is judged as making too much of an issue of the deviancy event or not and whether she was fair or not.

3. *Deviancy judgments.* These are judgments in which an evaluation of the teacher is not involved. The data for this dealt with the students' ratings of the seriousness of the misbehavior, and whether the student tended to take the deviant's side in the event.

THE DETERMINANTS OF TASK RELATED REACTIONS

The first set of hypotheses dealt with task related reactions to desists. *Task related ripple effects are determined by a student's commitment to learn the subject.* Whether a student pays more attention to the task or is inclined to behave better after witnessing a desist is determined by whether he has high motivation to learn the subject. *Desist qualities make no difference in this respect.* Students high in motivation to learn feel like behaving better and pay more attention to the task than students with low motivation to learn whether or not the desist contains punishment, firmness, anger, or humor. This is true whether or not they like the teacher.

Is there anything a teacher does by way of desisting that will influence the task related reactions of students with low motivation to learn? A teacher who desists is signalling her desire or intent to stop a misbehavior. She is saying "I want that stopped" for whatever reason she states or students think. One may also assume that the teacher's manner effects the intensity of the intent—that if she is angry, punishes, or is very firm, she is saying: "I *really* want that stopped!" Is there any group of students that is sensitive to, or influenced by a teacher's message signalling the intensity of her intent?

If a teacher signals a *strong* desire on her part to stop a misbehavior, does this make a difference? This makes a difference in only one of the four groups of students: the group having low motivation to learn with high liking for the teacher. If a student does *not* have a strong positive commitment to the task and *if* he likes the teacher, and *if* the teacher manifests a strong desire to have the misbehavior stop, then, and then only, will the student be more inclined to be more attentive and feel like behaving well himself.

THE DETERMINANTS OF REACTIONS INVOLVING EVALUATION OF TEACHERS

A second set of hypotheses dealt with those reactions to desists that related to evaluations of the teacher.

In order to understand these ripple effects we have applied Heider's theory of balance (6). Heider postulates forces to avoid imbalance and to maintain balance between our perceptions of people and their actions. We tend to see people we like as doing good things and people we dislike as doing bad things. These are balanced perceptions and are not conflicting. To perceive a liked person do a bad thing, or to perceive a disliked person do a good thing are imbalanced, conflicting units of perception.

One may assume that students perceive "being fair" as a "good" act and "being unfair" as a "bad" act. One can also assume that "making too much of an issue" of a misbehavior is "bad" and that "handling it just right" is "good." A balanced state of perception exists here if: (1) a liked teacher is seen as fair (or reacting right), and (2) a disliked teacher is perceived as unfair (or overreacting). An imbalanced state exists if: (1) a liked teacher is perceived as unfair (or overreacting), and (2) a disliked teacher is seen as fair (or reacting right).

The commitment to the teacher is the predominant determinant of students' evaluation of teachers' desists, when these evaluations have clear good-bad connotations. Comparisons between all four groups showed that students judged teachers for whom they had high liking as reacting with more appropriateness and with more fairness than teachers for whom they had low liking. This was true whether or not they were highly motivated to learn the subject.

Is there anything a teacher can do by way of desisting that will influence these evaluative judgments? The answer is: "nothing." In all four groups of students there was no difference between desists that did or did not contain anger, firmness, punishment, or humor. Regardless of the qualities of the teacher's desists, if a teacher is liked her desists are judged as "good" and if she is disliked they are judged as "bad." Differences in desist qualities are not of sufficient significance to change the evaluations produced by the prevailing commitment to the teacher, and this holds true for both high and low motivation to learn conditions.

THE DETERMINANTS OF JUDGMENTS RELATING TO THE DEVIANT AND THE DEVIANCY

What about evaluations of desist events that do not have clear connotations of good and bad? Balance theory would have liked persons to be perceived as doing "kind" things and disliked persons perceived as doing "mean" things, otherwise there would be conflict and imbalance. This is because "kind" and "mean" are important issues and are seen as "good" and "bad" respectively. However, disapproval of a liked person's tie may not produce a significant amount of conflict or imbalance, because the color of one's tie may not be important or carry strong good–bad connotations. Similarly, certain judgments about desist events may not have such strong good–bad connotations as judgments of fairness.

One of the judgments about a desist event had to do with whether the student tended to take the teacher's side, or the deviant's side. We assumed that taking a side was neither quite as important nor carried quite as much good–bad meaning as did fairness or unfairness. If this assumption is valid, then one should expect that taking the teacher's or deviant's side would follow balance theory and commitment to the teacher, but not as strongly as judgments of fairness. This proved to be the case.

Students' "taking sides" was affected only if *two* sets of conditions were met: liking for the teacher and her desisting in a strong manner. When teachers' desists contained punishment, anger, or strong firmness, students who liked her were more inclined to take the teacher's side and students who disliked her were more on the deviant's side. When the desist technique did not contain anger, punishment, or strong firmness, the students who liked her did not react differently from students who disliked her.

When making a judgment about an issue without strong good–bad values a student tends to take his cues from a teacher *if* he likes her and *if* she delivers a strong message. If he dislikes the teacher, then he does not take his cue from her when she does provide a clear cue. In fact, he may form an attitude opposite from her expressed feeling about the event.[2]

Another student judgment about the desist event related to how serious the student thought the deviancy was. This judgment is not clearly an evaluation of the teacher along good–bad dimensions. The teacher is not bad because the deviancy is serious, nor is she good because the deviancy is serious. And if the deviancy is not serious, this doesn't make the teacher good or bad either. There is no reason, therefore, for this judgment to follow balance theory closely. Consequently, one should *not* be able to predict students judgments of the seriousness of a deviancy from their liking for the teacher alone.

The judgment of the seriousness of a deviancy is not clearly a task related issue either, such as are attention or conformity. The perception of the degree of seriousness of a deviancy, then, is not clearly related to teacher evaluation (such as fairness) nor is it strongly related to task functions (such as attention). This means that students' judgments of the seriousness of a deviancy cannot be predicted from either their motivation to learn nor from their liking for the teacher alone. Is there *any* combination of commitments *and* desist qualities that will influence how students judge the degree of seriousness of a deviancy?

It was possible to predict students' judgments about the degree of seriousness of a deviancy. In order to do this, however, *three* sets of conditions had to be met. These were: (1) The student had to have low motivation to learn the subject (was not already slightly bending his judgment toward regarding a deviancy as serious); (2) the student had to like the teacher (was already inclined to be receptive to her messages); and (3) the teacher had to emit a *strong* message that she regards the deviancy as bad (by punishment, anger, or strong firmness). Thus, those students with low motivation

---

[2]Students did not report, a sufficient number of cases of deviancies committed by liked friends to check balance theory in relation to the deviant.

to learn witnessing a liked teacher desist in an intense manner were the only students who were influenced by the teachers in regard to judging these deviancies as serious ones. No other single commitment or combination of commitments or variations in desist qualities made a difference in how students judged the degree of seriousness of a deviancy.

THE QUESTIONNAIRE STUDY

A Questionnaire Study, modeled after the Interview Study, was conducted with beginning high school students. One purpose, in addition to replicating the Interview Study, was to see whether motivation to learn determined liking for a teacher. In order to check this, we obtained measures of students' intensity of "premotivation to learn world history" two weeks *prior* to their attendance in high school where all would be expected to take world history as an academic subject. The students were attending feeder schools for the high schools used in the interviews. World history was selected as the subject because of the wide range of degrees of motivation to learn expressed for this subject by students in the Interview Study.

Between one to two weeks after their beginning attendance at the high schools the students were administered questionnaires in their world history classes. These questionnaires, replicating the items in the Interview Study, had the students rate their motivation to learn the subjects they were taking, including world history. They were asked to describe the most recent incident in which the world history teachers attempted to stop some other student's misbehavior. Their descriptions of their reactions to the event were solicited as were their ratings for specific questions. Results were obtained from 280 students—146 boys and 134 girls.

There was some correlation ($r = .49$ for both boys and girls) between the motivation to learn scores obtained prior to their attendance in the high school (premotivation to learn) and their motivation to learn the world history course they were currently taking (post-motivation to learn). However, the premotivation to learn scores did *not* correlate with their liking for the world history teachers. Nor did these premotivation to learn scores correlate with *any other* reaction to the desist event: fairness, siding with teacher, attention just prior to the desist event, inclination to pay more attention to the task or to behave better or worse after the event, etc.

As found in the Interview Study, post-motivation to learn and liking for the teacher *were* significantly related. What is more, post-motivation to learn *did* relate to students' reactions to desist events, and these relationships were the same as those found in the Interview Study. Compared to students who were low in current motivation to learn, students who were high in current motivation to learn were more attentive to the task just prior to the desist, and were more inclined to pay even more attention to the task and to behave even better after the desist event.

The findings relating liking for teacher to students' reactions to desist events were also the same as those obtained in the Interview Study. Compared to students who had low liking for their current teachers, students who expressed high liking for their teachers rated the desist as more fair, were more inclined to take the teacher's side and saw the teacher as *not* making too much of an issue over the misbehavior.

Two qualities of desists studied in the interview were also studied in the questionnaires and similar results obtained in both studies. These were rated anger and firmness. (As might be expected, the written descriptions of the event given in the questionnaire were much more sparse than the oral descriptions given in the interviews. As a consequence, we did not feel able to reliably measure clarity, punishment, and harm to the deviant in the Questionnaire Study.) As found in the Interview Study, neither the presence of anger nor of strong firmness related to students' inclinations to pay more attention to the task or to behave better. The only relationship found between a desist quality as such and its impact upon the student was between teacher anger and a student's felt discomfort: When teachers manifested anger students felt uneasy or embarrassed.

The students were asked about two other issues that relate to liking for teachers and motivation to learn. These were: (1) *Task proficiency:* "How good is the teacher in 'getting the subject across'—in making it clear and interesting?" This was rated from "Not very good" to "Very, very good at it;" and (2) *Managerial proficiency:* "How good is the teacher in managing a class—in getting the class settled, working and behaving?" This was rated from "Not as good as average teacher" to "Much better than average teacher." Both of these ratings correlated with ratings of motivation to learn the subject and liking for the teacher. These correlations are presented in Table 3 and show that students' perceptions of teachers' task proficiency and managerial proficiency are associated with students' liking for a teacher and motivation to learn the subject. It might be noted that these proficiencies tend to be even *more* related to liking than to motivation to learn.

In general, it may be said that the Questionnaire Study supports the findings obtained in the Interview Study. In addition, the results indicate that motivation to learn is *not* determined solely by what a pupil brings to the class before his attendance in it, but is affected, even in one week, by what happens in the class and by whatever it is teachers do that leads to their being liked and to being perceived as being able to manage a class. In addition, motivation is influenced by the teacher's ability to explain and make a subject "interesting."

The high school interview was initiated in order to learn about students' reactions to desist events. We expected to find some relationships between desist qualities and ripple effects. Except for anger producing a feeling of discomfort, we found no relationship between desists, as such, and any kind of ripple effect. Instead, we

TABLE 3

Product Moment Correlations between Students' Ratings of Teachers and Students' Degree of Liking for Teacher and Degree of Motivation To Learn the Subject [a]

| | Motivation To Learn | | Liking for Teacher | |
	Boys	Girls	Boys	Girls
Ratings of Teachers	N=146	134	146	134
Task Proficiency	.33	.44	.65	.62
Managerial proficiency	.26	.30	.34	.45

[a] *r*'s of .25 and above are significant at the .01 level.

found that ripple effects were determined by the prevailing variables, predispositions, or commitments of motivation to learn and liking for the teacher.

What is more, motivation to learn and liking for teachers relate to different kinds of reactions to desist events. It is not a matter of an overall "halo effect." The commitment to learn determines task related ripple effects such as attention to the task and inclination to behave better or worse. Liking for the teacher determines evaluations of the event, such as fairness, that have good–bad connotations. If a student likes a teacher he judges her desist efforts as right and good and if a student dislikes a teacher he judges what she does as wrong or bad.

With the exception of anger producing a feeling of discomfort, desist qualities as such make no difference in the ripple effect except under very limited and special conditions. The special conditions require a particular combination of student predispositions, desist qualities, and kinds of judgments. The desist must contain a strong message of the teacher's attitude toward the deviancy by containing anger, punishment, or strong firmness; the student must have both a low motivation to learn and a high liking for the teacher; and the student's judgment must be about an issue that is not an evaluative judgment about the teacher. Thus, *if* the teacher's desist is intense, and *if* the student has low motivation to learn, and *if* the student likes the teacher, then the student will be inclined to judge the deviancy as serious and be inclined to pay more attention to the task.

WHAT STUDENTS SEE AS SALIENT ABOUT TEACHERS

Except for the relationship between anger and emotional discomfort, the high school studies showed that audience students' reactions to desist events were affected more by their commitments than by the qualities of the desists.

These findings lead to the question of what produces motivation to learn and liking for a teacher. Since no intensive observations of the classrooms involved were conducted, this question cannot be answered directly by the data. However, some indication of factors associated with these commitments might be obtained from the interview data.

During the interviews with the students we asked each student to describe each of the two teachers. The question asked was: "Suppose a friend of yours was trying to decide whether to get this teacher for this course. What would you tell him about this teacher? How would you describe this teacher?" This was asked for the high motivation to learn class and for the low motivation to learn class. The question was also asked in the second set of interviews conducted with the same students three months later. There are thus four separate descriptions by each student of specific, actual teachers.

What is it that students talk about when describing a specific teacher? What dimensions or attributes are most frequently mentioned and hence, apparently most salient? And are these saliencies different for high motivation and low motivation classes, and for high liked and low liked teachers?

These descriptions were coded and analyzed by Donald Keith Osborne (14). They were categorized as personal, managerial, and task attributes.

Personal attributes refer to descriptive statements having to do with a student's perception of the teacher as a person. Most of the categories are self explanatory. "Deviate teacher" is a report that the teacher is an odd or unusual person: "He's a nut;" "She's an odd ball;" "She's off her rocker." "Like teacher" or "dislike teacher" refer to descriptions which cannot be coded by any of the other personal categories but merely state that the student likes or dislikes the particular teacher: "She's nice;" "I like her;" "We have a mutual hate club—I hate him and he hates me."

Managerial attributes refer to statements about the teacher having to do with the student's perception of the teacher's style in handling behavior in the class. High tolerance refers to reports that the teacher has few rules and regulations, is easy going, and seldom punishes or enforces behavior rules. Low tolerance refers to a teacher who has many rules and is a strict enforcer.

Task attributes refer to a student's perception of the teacher as a task performer—with how the teacher handles the subject matter. Task approach ($+$) is coded when the student reports satisfaction with the teacher's method or approach to teaching the subject matter: "He reviews the material so we will understand;" "She stays on the subject;" "He uses slides and films;" "You can learn in his class." Task approach (−) refers to statements showing the student's dissatisfaction with the teacher's methods of handling the subject matter. Examples are: "He skips around too much;" "His lectures stink!" "He just gives written work, he won't discuss the material." Evaluation of demands refers to a student's statements that he approves or disapproves of the amount of task demands (homework and classroom) that the teacher makes.

The findings pertaining to the saliencies in students' perceptions of teachers are presented in Appendix 2.7 which summarizes the attributes spontaneously used by students when describing actual teachers. The results are presented for high motivation and low motivation classes as well as for high liked and low liked teachers.

The results provide some hints as to what kinds of teacher attributes students associate with motivation to learn as well as the kinds of attributes which are linked with the degree of liking for a teacher. Thus, for both high and low motivation to learn classes, liked teachers are described more frequently as being friendly or understanding than are disliked teachers; disliked teachers are described more frequently as being harsh, grouchy, and as having many enforced rules. More teachers in high motivation to learn classes are described as explaining the subject well, as using positive approaches to teaching the subject, and as making appropriate task demands; more teachers in the low learning classes are described as explaining the subject poorly and as using ineffective teaching methods.

It is especially noteworthy that students also differentiate between high and low liked teachers on the basis of task attributes. Liked teachers are described more as explaining well; disliked teachers more as explaining poorly. Further, liked teachers are described more as providing positive task approaches and as making more appropriate task demands than are low liked teachers. What the teachers actually *do* to lead to these perceptions is not, however, provided by these descriptions.

Of special significance is the preponderance of task attributes over personal attributes in descriptions of teachers. This is true for both high motivation to learn classes and for low motivation to learn classes, and for high liked as well as low liked teachers. Moreover, task saliencies outweigh personal saliencies even more during the third month of a class than during the first two weeks of a class. (What is more, the personal attributes mentioned include the innocuous statements of "liking," "disliking," and "neutral feelings" toward the teachers which are not descriptions in the true sense. If these were eliminated, the saliencies of personal attributes compared to task attributes would be even less.)

One might contrast these findings with a study by Polansky and Kounin(15) in which 150 adults and college students (clients) were asked to describe a professional helper (physician, social worker, college counselor) they had seen for the first time in a one-to-one relationship. The clients mentioned considerably more personal attributes when describing professional helpers (whether in a positive or negative manner) than did the students when describing teachers. Although the codes developed for the descriptions of teachers were different in specifics than the codes developed for the descriptions of professional helpers, it was possible to categorize the descriptions as task attributes or as personal attributes. (A managerial attribute was never given in the clients' descriptions.) Thus, "explained his diagnosis," "helped me gain insight," "helped me see my problem more clearly," could be categorized as task attributes. He was "friendly," "understanding," "a kind person," could be classified as personal attributes. When clients' descriptions were thus classified it was found that they mentioned 674 personal attributes of professional helpers and only 143 task attributes. This is a decided contrast to what students saw as salient about teachers, where only approximately 6 percent mentioned such personal attributes as "friendly," or "understanding," or "kind," and where mentions of task attributes outnumbered mentions of personal attributes.

Another contrasting finding should also be mentioned in this connection. In the Camp Study, campers were asked to describe their camp counselors. The most frequently used dimension was that which is called "gratuitous giver." Sixty-three percent of the campers (ranging from 7 to 13 years of age) used such statements as "gives us candy" and "brings us comic books" when describing their camp counselors. None of the high school students used this gratuitous giver category when describing teachers. Only 2.3 percent of the campers used terms that might be equivalent to task attributes ("taught us how to play ball better").

Evidently what students perceive as salient about teachers conducting a classroom is different from what campers perceive as salient about camp counselors or from what clients perceive as salient about professional helpers. And what is important in relation to being liked in one role is probably quite different from what leads to being liked in another. We suspect that what leads to being liked as a boyfriend or girlfriend, husband or wife, father or mother, is different from what is associated with being liked as a teacher. (The writer hopes that wives see husbands as likeable for other reasons than "being able to explain well" and as utilizing interesting methods of teaching an academic subject.) The findings from these studies strongly suggest that the behaviors categorized in studying teacher-student relationships must be unique to this role and not directly transposable from studies of other adult-child relationships, whether the latter be parents, psychotherapists, counselors, recreation directors, or others.

THE HIGH SCHOOL EXPERIMENT

An effort was made to replicate the findings of the High School Interview by means of controlled experiments.[3] Experimental manipulations were made of motivation to learn as well as of three types of desist techniques.

The schools that were feeder schools into the high schools used in the interviews were used to recruit participants in what was presented as a study of teaching methods. Students were offered $2.60 to come to the university campus for the research. A total of 246 students, 136 girls and 110 boys, were used in these experiments.

The scenario for the experiment was as follows:

1. After the students arrived at the campus and were seated in a classroom they were oriented to the study by one of the experimenters. The orientation included: explaining the procedure for their payment, asking them to assume that they were in a regular school classroom, informing them they were to see slides and hear tapes about Turkey and India to be conducted by an experienced teacher, and telling them they were to take a test on some of the material

---

[3]These experiments were planned and conducted by James J. Ryan, III, Paul V. Gump, and Jacob S. Kounin.

they were to see as well as to answer some questions about what they thought of how the lesson was conducted.

2. The teacher was introduced to the class and she, in turn, briefly introduced herself to them.

3. The teacher left the room and the experimenter handed out questionnaires to the students. The questionnaires consisted of two parts. The first part dealt with information about the student, such as grade level, marks received in Math and Social Studies, and how much they generally like Social Studies and Social Studies teachers. The second part dealt with their "first impressions" of the teacher they had just met which contained seventeen items corresponding to items used in the Interview Study.

4. *The manipulation of the degree of motivation to learn.* The experimenter told the students that they were to be given two lessons and two tests: one on Turkey and one on India. Some were told to pay high attention and try to learn as much as possible about Turkey, others about India. Which one they were to concentrate on was indicated by a card on their desk. (One half were given Turkey and one half India.) They were further told that they would all start with an extra $2.00, but that 10 cents would be taken away for each question they missed on the test *they* were to take. They were further told that if they were assigned Turkey to try *not* to pay attention to India as it would mix them up and result in their getting more things wrong about Turkey. (The India group was told *not* to attend to Turkey.)

5. The teacher returned and started to show the slides about Turkey and India and run the tape recorder. (These provided some major historical facts, geographical highlights, major economic bases, etc.)

6. A pretrained pupil misbehaved: got up, walked to the front of the room and proceeded to sharpen his pencil during the showing of the slides and playing of the recorded lesson.

7. *The manipulation of the desist techniques.* The teacher desisted the deviancy. One deviancy-desist event occurred per group. There were twelve groups, each group consisting of twenty to twenty-five pupils of both sexes and from different schools. Each type of desist was used for four different groups, and each group was assigned both high motivation and low motivation subjects. The teacher and the deviant were the same for all groups. The teacher

utilized three techniques of desisting the deviancy: (1) Punitive and angry (walked toward the deviant, saying: "Hey you, who do you think you are?" in a firm, irritated voice, put her arm on his shoulder in a gesture of pushing him into his seat, saying, "Now sit down! If you ever do that again, I'll really make trouble for you!"); (2) Simple reprimand (saying in a matter-of-fact tone: "Don't do that again. Please sit down in your seat now."); and (3) Ignoring (indicated awareness of the behavior, but merely stopped tape a moment, looked at him briefly, but did and said nothing).

    8. Lesson was resumed.

    9. Lesson was completed, and questionnaires were administered about the activities, the teacher, the deviancy event, and a test was given about Turkey and India.

Results Pertaining to the Desist Techniques

The "take" of the experimental manipulation of the desist techniques was evidenced by the existence of a significant difference between all groups in the predicted direction of the students' ratings of the teacher's meanness, anger, and degree of determination to stop the deviancy. The students who witnessed the punitive and angry desist technique did, in actuality, rate this as highest in meanness, anger, and firmness and the students witnessing the ignoring technique rated this as lowest in these qualities.

    Differences in desist techniques *did* make a difference in how audience students reacted to the desist event. Effects regarding judgments of the teacher were determined in two ways: changes in judgments about the teacher (differences between the first questionnaire about first impressions and the questionnaire administered later) as well as final judgments on the post-lesson questionnaire alone.

    Compared to the others, students witnessing the punitive and angry technique rated the deviancy as most serious, the degree of interference with attention to the lesson as greatest, the teacher as making too much of an issue over the event, the teacher as being best "able to maintain order in a class of *tough* kids," and the experience as producing most discomfort.

    Compared to the others, the simple reprimand resulted in the students reporting their paying more attention to the lesson following the event, and produced the highest ratings for teacher's fairness and for her being best "able to maintain order in *most* classes."

Students witnessing ignoring as the desist technique thought the misbehavior would be most likely to recur and rated the teacher as highest in her degree of liking for pupils.

Results Pertaining to Motivation To Learn

The final manipulation of the motivation to learn variable did produce a "take" by showing significant differences in rated degree of motivation to learn for the twelve groups between those assigned high motivation conditions and those assigned low motivation conditions.[4]

However, the degree of motivation to learn did not make a difference in the reactions of any of the students in any of the desist technique conditions. There were *no* differences between the high motivation students and the low motivation students in how they judged the deviancy, in their reactions to it (such as changes in attention), in their changes in judgments about the teacher, in their final judgments of the teacher, or in their judgments about the desist technique.

[4]Initially we were unable to produce differences between the high and low motivation to learn condition. In the first few trial experiments we offered $1 extra for good papers, 10 cents for each question correctly answered for the test that counted (Turkey for some, India for others), and told the subjects to concentrate only on the country of their assignment and *not* pay attention to the other. These instructions produced no difference in how much they reported they tried to learn the assigned lesson. The subjects were invited back by us, individually, to see if we could ascertain why our experimental induction of motivation did not "take." The typical answer was: "We figured that since this was a research study and you paid us for it, that we should do our best." It is only after we started with $2.00 extra and took away 10 cents for each mistake, and *strongly* emphasized that they should *not* pay attention to the unassigned part of the lesson because it would definitely get them mixed up, that the experimental manipulation of motivation to learn made a difference. This is mentioned here, since it does indicate what it may mean to be a "subject in an experiment" as compared to an actual student in a real classroom; to its relevance regarding the possible differences in kinds of findings that might be obtained by laboratory experiments compared to findings obtained by "naturalistic" or ecological methods of research. As the reader has probably already noticed, and as we will point out in further detail later, the findings we obtained about desist techniques are clearly different, partly depending upon whether we used laboratory experiments or ongoing classrooms to gather data.

Elizabeth Alden (1) also conducted experiments involving both prevailing variables about the teacher and desist technique variables. Both sets of variables related to the general dichotomy derived from descriptions of teachers in terms of personal and task attributes. Specifically, in her study, the personal saliency of the teacher was developed by focusing upon her warmth and liking for children; the task saliency was enhanced by focusing upon her expertness in the task. Correspondingly, the desist techniques were categorized as having either an approval focus (". . . I don't like it when. . .") or a task focus (". . . you can't learn this if . . .").

The findings of the Alden experiment parallel those of the High School Experiment in spite of the fact that she used subjects of a different age (5th graders), different tasks, different prevailing variables, and different desist techniques. In both experiments the prevailing variables did *not* influence the ripple effect, whereas the desist techniques did. Alden found that the prevailing variables of teacher's expertness and teacher's liking for children did not make a difference, whereas her desist techniques did, with the task-focus techniques producing clearly more favorable ripple effects than the approval-focus techniques.

The findings of Alden demonstrating the greater effectiveness of task-focus over approval-focus desist techniques may well be contrasted with a group of experiments by Kounin, Polansky, Biddle, Coburn, and Fenn (3, 4, 5, 11) involving experiments of initial interviews between counselors and college students. In the latter experiments, as in Alden's, audience students witnessed an initial interview of a college student with a professional counselor. The counselors behaved in different manners in certain points of the interview, and students' reactions to these different styles of counseling were measured. Three different experiments were conducted with three different sets of scripts. In all three experiments, however, comparisons were made between what were categorized as relationship-centered styles of counselor behavior and problem-centered styles of counselor behavior. Though differing in detail, the relationship-centered style is equivalent to Alden's approval-focus and Osborne's personal attributes; and the problem-centered style is equivalent to Alden's task-focus and Osborne's task attributes. Contrary to Alden's study where a clear superiority is evident for the use of task-focus rather than approval-focus techniques, the experiments on the initial interviews with professional counselors demonstrated a clear superiority of relationship-centered styles over problem-centered styles. Compared to college students who witnessed counselors focusing more on problem-centered behaviors, students who witnessed counselors manifesting more relationship-centered behaviors (but not anti-problem or ignore-problem behavior) were more inclined to return for further interviews, felt more progress, felt more at ease, felt more like communicating to the counselor, etc. The reader might also recall, at this point, that students describing real teachers mention task attributes more than personal attributes, and that clients describing real professional helpers mention personal attributes more than problem attributes.

Considering the milieu differences obtained in the Superego Study; the differences in saliencies found between descriptions of teachers and descriptions of other professional helping persons; and the differences between the reactions of subjects in experiments to equivalent behavior-styles dependent upon whether they were reacting to teachers in a classroom or to counselors in a one-to-one relationship; we were forced more and more to conclude that one must study real teachers in actual classrooms in order to learn about managerial techniques, or any other aspects of teacher-pupil relationships.

PART II:

THE VIDEOTAPE STUDIES OF DIMENSIONS OF CLASSROOM MANAGEMENT

3

THE VIDEOTAPE STUDY: THE DEATH OF THE DESIST TECHNIQUE ISSUE

THE PRESENT STATUS OF THE DESIST PROBLEM

At this point let us take stock of the findings about desist events up to this time. This will not only furnish a perspective of the research findings but will highlight some questions about them, and serve to provide a rationale for the major study that is to follow.

A major question is whether or not desist techniques, as such, make any difference in how students react. Does a teacher's technique of handling a misbehavior make any difference in how students who are audience to this event react? Do differences in desist techniques produce different effects upon attitudes or overt behavior? Is one technique more effective than another?

Anger and Punitiveness

The only quality of a desist technique that shows a consistent effect in all the studies conducted is that of anger and punitiveness. (1) In the observations conducted in kindergartens during the first week of school, it was found that when teachers desisted a misbehavior with roughness (anger and/or punitiveness, but mostly anger) that audience pupils reacted with more behavior disruption (overt signs of apprehension or anxiety, restlessness, less involvement in the ongoing task) than when teachers desisted without roughness. (2) In both the High School Interview and the High School Questionnaire Studies, students who witnessed a desist containing anger reported more emotional discomfort than when they witnessed a desist that did not contain anger. (3) A similar finding obtained in the High School Experiment. (4) In a study of first-grade children using the Superego questions (9), children who had punitive teachers gave markedly different responses in an interview about misbehavior than children who had nonpunitive teachers. (See Appendix 3.1) Compared with children who had nonpunitive teachers, children with punitive teachers manifested more conflict about classroom behavior, were less concerned about school-unique matters, and were more preoccupied with aggression. (One might point out that punitiveness related not only to misbehavior and desist events, but was a general teacher mode of behavior that was also applied to issues other than misbehavior, such as making mistakes in work.)

Differences between Experimental and Field Studies

There were crucial differences between the findings obtained when using subjects in experiments and the findings obtained when using students in existing classrooms.

In *all* the experiments, differences in qualities of desist techniques *made a difference* in how audience students reacted. In the College Experiment, students who witnessed a threatening technique reacted differently than students who witnessed a supportive technique. In the High School Experiment, there were differences between the reactions of students dependent upon whether they witnessed a desist technique that was punitive/angry, a simple reprimand, or consisted of deliberate ignoring. The Alden Experiment demonstrated that upper elementary school pupils reacted differently to desists that were task-focused than to desists that were approval-focused.

On the other hand, in *none* of the experiments did the manipulation of prevailing variables make any difference in how audience students reacted to desist events. In the High School

Experiment, students in high motivation to learn conditions reacted the same to desist events as did students in low motivation to learn conditions. In Alden's experiments, pupils reacted the same to desist events both when the teacher's liking for children was highlighted as well as when the teacher's expertness in the subject was emphasized.

In contrast, the field studies showed that prevailing variables *were* the significant determinants of persons' reactions to desist events and that desist qualities, as such, were *not*. Both the High School Interview and the High School Questionnaire showed that students' reactions to desists that contained punishment, anger, clarity, firmness, and humor were no different from their reactions to desists that did not have these qualities. The Camp Study also showed that desist qualities made no difference in how campers behaved following their witnessing desist events. On the other hand, the High School Interviews and the High School Questionnaires demonstrated that prevailing variables (commitments) did relate to reactions to desist events regardless of the qualities of the desists. The prevailing variables studied were motivation to learn and liking for the teacher. Motivation to learn predicted to task related reactions of students (attention to task, inclination to behave well) and liking for the teacher predicted to evaluative reactions (fairness, overreacting).

There is no doubt then, that the findings about desist events obtained from experiments are different from those obtained from field studies. One cannot even answer the question of which studies are right. Insofar as the studies were carefully conducted one must say that both are "right" at this point in the inquiry. Opinions and theories about behavior management in classrooms, however, may be quite different, or contradictory, depending upon which sets of findings one selects to emphasize. Implications for classroom management and for problems of discipline will certainly differ depending upon whether one chooses to place faith in the findings of the experiments or in the findings of the field studies. Do desist techniques make a difference in classrooms or do they not? Do the kinds and qualities of prevailing variables make the difference? Is classroom management and discipline a matter of the appropriate selection and use of desist techniques or a matter of the use of techniques (not ascertained so far in these researchers) relating to prevailing variables and commitments?

Some Ecological Considerations

Instead of attempting to decide whether the results of the experiments or the results of the field studies are the correct or crucial findings, one may conclude that all findings are correct, but for different reasons. Similarly, one may conclude that the findings from the Kindergarten Study (where desist techniques made a difference, and mostly on the first day of school) and the Camp Study (where desist techniques did not make a difference) are also both "correct" findings, but for different reasons. Both of the latter, one might note, are field studies.

The different reasons may lie in *ecological realities*. What is it like to be a subject in an experiment, a camper in a cabin clean-up activity, or a pupil in a classroom during a recitation period? What is salient and important enough to make a difference in one setting may be quite different from what is salient and important in another.

Even within the experimental method, where one attempts to simulate real life variables, one may have to be sensitive about the degree of ecological realism of the variables. In this connection one should recall the element of surprise that was reported by the subjects who witnessed a college professor desisting a student. This ecological strangeness of desisting a student in college may well have been as important or more important than the experimental variable and may have gone unheeded and unrecorded by an experimenter. This element of surprise was *not* reported by the students in the High School Experiment. Evidently the use of desists is not ecologically strange or unexpected in high school classrooms, but is in college classrooms.

Important variables that influence the behaviors studied may also be neglected in field studies of naturally occurring and nonmanipulated events. Thus, in the High School Interview Study, where motivation to learn as a prevailing variable influencing reactions to desist events was focused upon, we would have formed different conclusions depending upon whether or not we happened to have measured liking for the teacher as a coexisting prevailing variable.

The importance of ecological factors is especially relevant in the issue of misbehavior management, which is the focus of these researches. This is evident in the results of the Superego Studies where children were questioned about misconduct. Their preoccupations and perceptions regarding misconduct differed depending upon whether they were talking about home, camp, or school. These were across-the-board differences. The differences among these settings applied to the type of misconducts (physical assault, disobedience, etc.), the targets of these misconducts (peers, objects, central adults, etc.), and the role of the central adult as either target or retributor (kinds of suffering, kinds of acting-back on the one who misbehaved, etc.).

The attributes around which a person perceives a central adult (camp counselor, teacher, professional helper in a one-to-one relationship) are also dependent upon ecological factors (which include the role of the central person). Thus, descriptions of actual camp counselors contain the most mentions of gratuitous giver (brings watermelons); descriptions of real teachers contain the most mentions of task attributes (explains well, gets off the track); and descriptions of actual professional helpers contain the most mentions of relationship attributes (friendly, understanding). Regardless of whether the attributes mentioned are true or not, the differences in the nature of the descriptions do indicate that persons perceive different behaviors and attributes as salient; that some qualities and behaviors are more important than others; and that major global judgments or commitments ("I like," "I recommend," "I'll accept influence from") are formed around different perceived attributes, behaviors, or techniques, dependent upon ecological factors of settings and the position of their key personnel.

The conclusion that perceived saliencies and related judgments and commitments are dependent upon different behaviors in different settings is further supported by findings from experiments. In first-contact experiments, Alden found that pupils who witnessed task-focus behaviors of teachers formed more favorable judgments and were more influenced by the teacher than pupils who witnessed teachers who utilized approval-focus techniques. In contrast, and also in first-contact experiments, students who witnessed professional counselors utilizing more relationship-centered techniques formed more favorable judgments and made more positive commitments to those counselors than students who witnessed counselors who engaged more exclusively in problem-centered behaviors.

Obviously, the classroom setting is different in many respects (as well as similar in some) from a camp cabin, a recreation center, a counselor's office, or a home. The classroom has its own ecology. It has geographical location, physical setting, props, activities, time allotments, personnel, events, expectations, and purposes that make it different in many respects from other settings. And being a pupil in a classroom is not the same as being a patient in a doctor's office or a subject in an experiment. And being a teacher is different from being a parent, doctor, recreation leader, or experimenter.

If this is so, then it means that one must be cautious in applying research findings from experiments or from studies of other adult-child relationships to the behavior of children in classrooms, or to teachers, without first validating them in the realities of classrooms. This does not mean that the findings from experiments or from other settings are not valid. It does mean that the variables that may be significant in an experiment may be so outweighed in importance by certain ecological variables that the former just don't make a noticeable difference in classrooms.

The necessity for studying actual classrooms is especially important for problems of discipline when this is defined as a problem of behavior management. We need to know what teachers *do* that makes a difference in how pupils behave in classrooms. Not only do we need to know more about what teachers do to manage misbehavior when it occurs, but we must know what they do to develop commitments to learn, to behave, or to becoming "liked" or "recommended" in their position as classroom teachers. So far, we don't even know for certain whether their desist styles make a difference or not.

THE RATIONALE OF THE VIDEOTAPE STUDY

At this point in our researches about behavior management in classrooms we were left with as many questions as answers. Apparent differences in findings about desist events obtained in different settings, or with different methods of research, forced us into an ecological frame of reference. In order to make more certain that important variables were not overlooked in favor of unimportant ones (no matter how testable and statistically significant these latter might be in experiments) we decided that a naturalistic, ecologically-oriented approach was called for; i.e., the study of many coexisting events in real settings. Our further research in behavior management in classrooms was then to be conducted in a spirit of inquiry to see what could be learned rather than in a spirit of debate to see what hypothesis or theory was to be tested.

With a focus upon "emotionally disturbed" children in regular classrooms, Dr. A. E. Norton and the writer spent several months observing approximately 100 different elementary school classrooms containing what principals, teachers, and school diagnosticians labeled as emotionally disturbed children. We were always armed with pencils and notebooks in addition to our own senses. At different times, we were accompanied by experts from fields other than our own—curriculum, elementary school methods, guidance, social group work.

At the end of several months we had accumulated some impressions and several filled notebooks but had very little scientific data that would enable us to fill in some numbers in a simple table of results pertinent to the question of behavior management in classrooms.

The main difficulty behind the failure to obtain useable data pertinent to the research problem was the inadequacy of the data-gathering medium—the human observer. Some of our deficiencies as data-gathering media were:

1. *An inability to obtain complete records of what happened.* In spite of many combinations of divided responsibilities in record taking and synchronization, we were never satisfied that our records contained *all* that happened. We may have recorded, with a reasonable degree of completeness and objectivity, the behavior of one child in the manner of Barker-Wright's (2) specimen records. But there is more than the behavior of one child to be considered in an ecological study of a classroom. At a minimum, there are activities, props, other children, and a teacher.

The behavior of the teacher was especially impossible to record with any satisfactory degree of completeness. Teachers simply have a large behavior volume—they do many different things, in many ways, and direct these behaviors at too many targets, to allow an observer to record their behavior with completeness.

2. *A tendency to selectively notice and record events that were impressive, contrasting, in line with some pre-existing hypotheses or concerns, intense, or otherwise perceptually outstanding to the point of the exclusion of other mundane and less noticeable events.* Thus, if a child was tossing paper airplanes in the air at the back of the room, this event would be in our notes. However, the notes would contain little description of what the other children were doing—for instance, that when eighteen children were supposedly engaged in "think and do" seatwork, sixteen of the eighteen were writing in their workbooks, one child glanced at the deviant for two seconds and resumed writing in his workbook, and one child looked at the airplane-tosser with apparent interest, removed a sheet of paper from his desk, and started to make a paper airplane.

3. *A propensity to include labels, evaluations, judgments, pseudointerpretations, summaries, and other types of nonobjective and nondescriptive entries.* To write that children are "attentive," "well-behaved," "disorderly," "apathetic," and the like, is not to provide descriptions of actual behaviors. These are judgments made by an observer and are not behavior facts.

4. *An inclination to arrive at premature interpretations about the management of children's behavior.* An example from the notes: The teacher was reading the story with high enthusiasm, changing voice inflection and "hamming it up," paused, leaned forward in her seat, and visually swept all the children in the reading group, and said: "The next part is a *real* surprise. What do you think he'll find under his bed?", looked around suspensefully and then. . . all the children were waving their hands to be called on, including five "preemies" (children who raised their hands even before the questions was asked). . .

In addition to an incomplete description, our notes contained the interpretation that these teachers who are enthusiastic and suspenseful produce enthusiasm in children. A few days later we would observe a teacher who was labeled as matter-of-fact and calm, and who simply raised a question while remaining seated in her chair. Children waved hands "enthusiastically" to be called on, including six "preemies". . . . . . What happened to our previous interpretation that enthusiasm in children is produced by enthusiasm in teachers? Evidently there must be something else that both teachers are doing, or that is occurring, which is less noticeable than the histrionics, and that has the effect of inducing X-degree of volunteering on the part of children.

The above, as well as additional inadequacies in the records of events and behaviors in classrooms, led us to conclude that answers to the kinds of questions one might raise about classroom management require a better data-gathering medium than the human observer. Such a data-gathering medium must record *all* events that occur in a classroom whether perceptually intense or barely noticeable, whether interesting or dull, or whether supportive or nonsupportive of a particular theory or point of view. These events must include activities, children, and teacher. Moreover, the data-gathering method should not only provide factual bases for measuring preselected events (i.e., desist events) or provide ways of checking existing hypotheses, but should also provide data for ideas or hypotheses not thought of at the time of data-gathering. It should provide data that would allow for repeated study of the same events by different persons. These criteria would preclude check lists, rating scales, and other secondary data. For, once the ratings are made, the original events are over and no longer available for study. All that remains are the ratings that are preselected and sifted out from many other events by the original observer.

We decided to use videotapes. The combination of a lens and videotape recording meets the criteria of a good observer and recorder. The lens has no biases, theories, preconceptions, needs, or interests. It takes in all that is occurring in its field and makes no distinctions between what is boring or interesting, major or minor, important or unimportant, outstanding or ordinary, good or bad. And the videotape records it all without forgetting, exaggerating, theorizing, judging, interpreting, or eliminating.

Two TV cameras were mounted in boxes and placed on stands in a classroom. One camera was placed in a position to record the largest possible area of the classroom continuously and without editing or selecting. The second camera, equipped with a remote-controlled pan-tilt mechanism, enabled the engineer, at the direction of the project director, to record various positions in the classroom and to superimpose this picture on some part of the major picture that would not conceal the behaviors shown on it. Priority was given to videotaping the teacher and next the emotionally disturbed children when they were lost from the main picture. Two microphones were used to record sound—the main source being a wireless transmitting microphone worn by the teacher that produced a recording of everything she said on the videotape. All recording was accomplished by remote-control using equipment in a truck parked outside the school building.[1]

Since this research pertains to the management of overt behavior, the behavior of the children was coded for work involvement and deviancy. Managerial success in a classroom is defined as producing a high rate of work involvement and a low rate of deviancy in academic settings.

Only behavior in academic activities (reading, arithmetic, social studies, science, etc.) was scored. Children's behavior during nonacademic activities (attendance, milk time, nonacademic games, etc.) was not coded. Scores were kept separately for seatwork settings (where children engage in some kind of seatwork without direct supervision by the teacher) and recitation settings (where the teacher is actively engaged in conducting some sort of recitation with an entire class or subgroup of children).

Wherever possible, the behavior of eight nondisturbed children was coded for each academic activity in addition to the behavior of the emotionally disturbed children. The children were selected from each of the four quadrants of the seating arrangement during the activity. Scores were kept separately for the emotionally disturbed children.

The behavior of the child preselected for coding was categorized every ten seconds for the duration of the activity. Following

[1]In a preliminary Videotape Study, thirty self-contained classrooms from predominantly middle-class suburbs were videotaped continuously for one half day each. The classrooms were videotaped during the months of March and April, or at the eighth and ninth months of their formation. Fifteen first- and second-grade classrooms were videotaped in Suburb X and fifteen classrooms from grades three through five were videotaped in Suburb Y. The only basis for the selection of a classroom was that it contain at least one emotionally disturbed child as diagnosed by professionals in a psychiatric clinic.

The results pertaining to the management of the emotionally disturbed children are presented in Kounin and others (8) and Kounin & Obradovic (7). Since the results regarding the management of these children are no different from the results pertaining to management of the nondisturbed children, they will not be presented separately here.

this, the behavior of another child was scored, and so on until the behavior of all the preselected children was scored. (The children were preselected by the project director on the basis of a seating chart plus visibility on the screen.)

The behavior categories were:

1. Definitely and completely involved in work (DI)
2. Probably involved in work (PI)
3. Definitely not involved in work (DO)
4. Restless
5. Languishing
6. Engaged in task related deviancy (TR)
7. Engaged in nontask related deviancy (NTR)

The latter was further divided into mild, and serious deviancies. Whenever an emotionally disturbed child engaged in an NTR, the behavior of the children around him or her was further coded in order to obtain a measure of deviancy contagion–of how much the misbehavior of a disturbed child affected the behavior of the children around him.

The major results had to do with a teacher's degree of managerial success. Three such scores were used: (1) work involvement rate. This was the average of the children's DI/DO ratios; (2) deviancy rate. This was obtained from the number of ten-second intervals in which an NTR occurred. A mild deviancy was scored one and a serious deviancy was scored two. (Fewer than 1 percent of the intervals contained a serious deviancy such as overt aggressive acts or open defiance of a teacher, and these were found in but five of the classrooms.) (3) Contagion rate. This was the mean percentage of children in the vicinity of an emotionally disturbed child who entered into a deviancy initiated by him.

Since there were significant differences between the scores obtained in seatwork and those obtained in recitation (with more managerial success in recitation) results were analyzed separately.

RESULTS REGARDING DESIST TECHNIQUES

The first question we attempted to answer was whether or not desist techniques make a difference in children's reactions to desist events. Does the manner in which a teacher handles a misbehavior affect the behavioral reactions of a child to this event or not?

A desist code was developed that dealt with this issue. One might call these "direct" managerial techniques—the techniques of dealing with misbehavior as such. Every time a teacher did something to stop a child's misbehavior, the incident was coded for how the teacher did it and for the degree of success she had in stopping that misbehavior.

The degree of success for stopping the misbehavior was coded on a seven-point scale. In the case of a desist, we assume that a teacher not only wants the child to *stop* his misbehavior, but, whether she says so or not, also wants him to *do* whatever is the legal task at the time. That is, "stop talking" also means "get to work." The scale for desist success was as follows:

1. Immediate, quick, eager, and enthusiastic conformity. The target quickly stops the deviancy and also gets with the legal activity hurriedly.
2. Same as 1 but not quite. The target stops the deviancy quickly but unhurriedly starts the legal activity.
3. Ordinary conformity and obedience. The target stops the deviancy immediately but slowly and laggingly gets with the legal activity.
4. Same as three but not quite. Normal conformity for the cessation of deviancy but not getting with the legal activity.
5. Resistance shown. The stopping of deviancy is only partial (reduces intensity of misbehavior only, but still somewhat misbehaving) or very slow, and does not start any legal activity.
6. Same as five but not quite. More defiant than compliant.
7. Open defiance. The deviancy continues in the same manner or with more intensity.

The reaction of the child to the teacher's desist was scored for the immediate impact as well as for the impact for 10 seconds.

The desist techniques were coded for their clarity, firmness, intensity, focus, and child treatment. These are exemplified in the code explained in the following paragraphs.

Clarity

In clarity (as in the Kindergarten Code) the coders sought to categorize how much literal (not by inference) information the desist contained. From the point of view of the child who would be looking at the teacher at that moment, does the desist contain, either by actual words or by definite signals (looking or pointing directly at, motioning to "sit," finger to mouth with a "shh") the following information?

1. Who is deviant? ("Johnny" rather than "somebody.")
2. What to *stop* doing? ("Stop talking" rather than "stop.")
3. What to *do*? ("Take your seat," "Get to your work," or use of a model: "I like the way Mary is sitting.")
4. Why? ("You're disturbing others," "You might trip and get hurt.")
5. Nagging. A distinction was made between nagging and clarity. A nag consisted of a teacher bombarding or "lecturing" with content or reasons beyond which the child may be presumed to already know quite well. A nag was defined as producing a reaction on the part of the child of "O.K., O.K., I know already!"

Firmness

Firmness means the degree to which the teacher conveys an "I-mean-it" and a "now!" in her desist order. Part of firmness comes from the manner she uses in sending out her message and part of firmness comes from her follow-through once the message is issued.

The message part has a "clarity" aspect: does the desist order make a clear break from the previous activity? Is it clear, precise, sharp, and have a good figure-ground contrast (all conveying a "right now!")? This is conveyed by the teacher making a clear break from her previous geographical position, stopping her previous activity, emitting a warning signal ("In a minute I'll. . ."), and using a tone of voice that stands out.

The reverse is "wishy-washy" and hesitant, conveyed by remaining half-in or half-returning to the previous activity, communicating uncertainty ("Well, let's see now," "I guess. . .").

The message-clarity part of firmness was coded as:

1. High: If the teacher used two or more of the above clarity manners.
2. Ordinary: If she used one of the above clarity manners.
3. Hesitant: If she used none of the above clarity manners or if any of the anti-clarities were present.

The follow-through aspect of firmness entails the following behaviors: moving closer to deviant, looking at firmly during and for a while after the issuance of the order, using a "physical assist" (leading by arm, holding, moving a chair or prop), using a "repeat urge" that is *not* a repeat in response to a failure.

The follow-through part of firmness was scored as:

1. High: If she used two or more of the above behaviors.
2. Some: If she used one of the above behaviors.
3. None: If she used none of the above or had the opposite (such as immediately turning to something else before the desist was settled).

Harassed was coded to distinguish a "fake" firmness from a real firmness (much as "nagging" was distinguished from clarity). It is a desist in which the teacher is "beaten" and is "giving up." Thus she shows anger, raises her voice, or bombards with repeat orders either because her desist has already failed or because she shows she really doesn't expect conformity.

Intensity

Intensity refers to the intensity of the stimulus quality of the desist: its attention-demanding properties and its potential to intrude into the awareness of audience children.

1. Low: A desist signal that doesn't contrast with the background activity (little, if any, change in teacher position or manner) and is of low intensity and short duration. An audience child would have to be watching the teacher at the time to be aware of it.
2. Medium: A desist that has moderate contrast (geography, tone) or moderate intensity but is short.
3. High: Has medium contrast but is long in duration; or has high stimulus intensity; or contains affect laden material (sarcasm, real threat). An audience child would have to be blind and deaf not be made aware of it.

Focus

Focus refers to what the teacher concentrates upon in her desist order. By inference, if not by explicitly stated content, behavior orders have a *desist* or stop ("stop talking") content and an *induction* or begin ("work on your arithmetic") content. Which is the teacher focusing on? The deviancy part or the induction part? Or both?

If the teacher remains focused on the child's misbehavior and does nothing explicitly to get him into the legal activity it is coded as a deviancy focus. If she deals only with the legal activity in her desist it is coded as an induction focus ("Johnny, do your arithmetic problems"). If she deals with both ("If you stop talking you'll finish your arithmetic") it is coded as having both a deviancy focus and an induction focus because the teacher not only directs him to get *out of* the deviancy region (talking) but also *into* the induction region (arithmetic). The coders also determined whether the teacher added a negative quality to the deviancy ("If you keep talking I'll give you an E in citizenship") or to the induction ("You'll fail your arithmetic"), or to both. They also coded whether the teacher added a positive quality to the deviancy ("If you stop talking you'll get a gold star") or to the induction (". . . if you finish your arithmetic you'll get a gold star"), or to both.

Thus, the focus of a desist could be on deviancy only, with a positive, negative, or neutral quality; on the induction only, with a positive, negative, or neutral quality; or on both, with the respective qualities for either.

Child Treatment

This part of the code dealt with how the child was treated in the desist. Does the child see the teacher as being for or against him in this incident?

1. Pro-child or Positive: If the teacher's manner is such as to be seen by the child as protecting him against harm then this would be coded as pro-child. (This might have negative focus, but the manner might be pro-child. "You might get hurt if you fight," could be pro-child even though there is harm in the content, if the teacher communicates an intent to protect him from being hurt. "I don't want you to fail," may be negative in focus but pro-child here.) "Cushions" ("You may play later"), and other attempts to protect the feelings of a child would be coded as pro-child. Rewards, compliments, and praises

would, of course, be coded pro-child. (It was rare to find a teacher who praised a child for deviancy. Teachers just don't say, "My, but isn't it nice that Johnny hit Mary.")

2. Anti-child or Negative: This category was the equivalent of roughness in the Kindergarten Study and of anger/-punitiveness in the High School Studies. Manifest negative feelings toward the deviant (anger, sarcasm) as well as threats and punishments were coded as anti-child.

3. Neutral: These were desists that contained neither negative nor positive child treatments.

Each desist for every teacher was coded for each of the above qualities.

Having developed reliable measures of both desist techniques and of children's behaviors we are now in a position to answer the question of whether variations in desist techniques make any difference in the behavior of children. There are two methods of ascertaining the relationship between desist techniques and managerial success with the data available. One method is to see whether, for any one teacher, there is a relationship between her desist technique and her degree of success in handling a particular deviancy. Another is to see whether teachers who differ in their general style of handling deviancies have different degrees of general managerial success.

The first method asks the question : Does Miss Smith have more success in handling a deviancy when desisting with Quality X than she does when desisting without Quality X? Does Miss Smith have the same degree of success when she handles a deviancy with Quality Y as she does when she doesn't include Quality Y? Is the same true for Miss Pretty and Miss Ugly, for Miss Young and Mrs. Old, for Mrs. Fat and Miss Thin, Miss Kind and Miss Mean, and for all the other teachers?

An answer to the above kind of question was obtained by correlating a specific teacher's scores for each of her desists with her scores for the degree of success in handling each of the corresponding deviancies. When Miss Smith utilizes a desist technique that is high in clarity does she produce a higher degree of conformity than when she uses a low clarity technique? When she is firm is she more successful than when she is not? A similar question was asked for Miss Smith for the qualities of focus, intensity, and child treatment. The same questions were answered for each of the other twenty-nine teachers and for each of the five desist qualities measured. Two types of measures of immediate success were also utilized: immediate response and response for 10 seconds.

This produced 300 different correlations: 30 teachers x 5 desist qualities x 2 measures of the degree of success. There were only two correlations that were significant at the .05 level—a result that can be obtained by chance alone. The remaining 298 correlations were insignificant. One must conclude that *there is no relationship between the qualities of a teacher's desist techniques and the degree of her success in handling a deviancy.* Thus, for any one teacher, neither the degree of clarity, firmness, and intensity of her desist effort; nor whether she focuses on the misbehavior, or on the legal activity, or on both; nor whether she treats the child positively, negatively, or neutrally; makes any difference for how readily a child stops his deviancy or gets with the prescribed task.

Another method of seeing whether desist techniques make any difference in how children behave is to correlate teachers' average scores for desist techniques with their scores for managerial success. Thus, all of a teacher's desist scores for clarity, intensity, firmness, focus, and child treatment were averaged. Each teacher would thus be scored for the general degree of clarity, firmness, etc. of her desists. These scores were correlated with three scores of managerial success: work involvement, deviancy rate, and the degree of deviancy contagion. There were also two sets of scores for work involvement and deviancy rate: one set for the emotionally disturbed children and one for the nondisturbed children. These scores were further separated for seatwork activities and for recitation activities.

None of the correlations between teachers' desist styles and managerial success were significant. This finding held true for the emotionally disturbed children as well as for the nondisturbed children, and for seatwork settings as well as for recitation settings. As far as this research is concerned, it must be concluded that *the techniques of dealing with misbehavior, as such, are not significant determinants of how well or poorly children behave in classrooms, or with how successful a teacher is in preventing one child's misbehavior from contaging others.*

CONCLUSIONS REGARDING DESIST TECHNIQUES AS AN ISSUE IN CLASSROOM MANAGEMENT

The findings from the Videotape Study that desist techniques are not significant determinants of managerial success in classrooms is consistent with the findings from the High School Interview Study, the High School Questionnaire Study, and (although it did not deal with classrooms) the Camp Study. These studies all demonstrated that ripple effects were unrelated to the desist technique used by the adult in charge but *were* related to prevailing variables. One might also say that this general conclusion is also true of the Kindergarten Study where there were considerably more "no observable effects" consequent to desist events during the second through fourth day than on the first day of school.

In contrast, all the experiments that were conducted demonstrated that the ripple effect was dependent upon differences in the teachers' desist techniques. This was true for the College Experiment, the High School Experiment, and Alden's experiment with fifth graders. Desist techniques also made a difference in the behaviors of kindergarten children on the first day in school. Why the difference between these studies and the others?

The differences might be partly attributable to the differences between being a subject in an experiment and a student in an actual classroom. In this connection one might note the difficulty we experienced in experimentally creating the prevailing variable of low motivation to learn in the High School Experiment. In the experiment, the subjects had the commitment of doing their best as subjects in an experiment—a commitment that the experimenters had to try very hard to overcome. This explanation, however, would not account for the finding that desist techniques apparently do make a difference on the first day of kindergarten where we were dealing with real pupils in real classrooms.

A more plausible explanation for the differences between the experiments and the other studies may pertain to the fact that the experiments all involved first contacts with the experimental teacher. We are inclined to feel that the experimenters were deceived more than the subjects by the reasons we gave them for conducting the studies. Our statements to the subjects that we were studying first impressions of teachers is probably closer to the truth than our hidden purpose of studying desist techniques.

If this is so, then the experiments were dealing with variables relating to the social psychology of first impressions rather than to the ripple effect of desist techniques. The fact, for example, that students reacted differently to a punitive desist technique than to a nonpunitive desist technique may only be accidentally related to the issue of discipline. Any other kind of punitive event may have produced similar reactions on the part of witnessing students. The experimental teachers may have acted punitively or nonpunitively to a cat that walked into the room, or to a student for having a mustache, and audience students may have reacted differently to these events in much the same manner that they reacted differently to desist events.[2]

The conclusion that desist styles are not significant determinants of behavior management in classrooms does not mean that misbehavior in classrooms is not an important issue and is not of genuine concern to teachers when it occurs. As a matter of fact, concern with discipline techniques may be as prevalent as it is because misbehavior does stand out perceptually. While observing a classroom, one is more likely to notice a child who is throwing crayons than a child who is going about the business of writing in his workbook. And a teacher who is reprimanding a pupil is more likely to be noticed than when she is listening to a child read. Furthermore, there is no questioning the fact that one may observe a desist technique that is effective as well as observe a desist technique that is ineffective, especially if these occur in different classrooms. Thus, we have seen Teacher A walk to the light switch and flick the lights on and off two times as a signal for the children to be quiet and listen to her. It worked. The children immediately stopped talking or doing whatever they were doing, and sat in a posture of attention facing the teacher. Is this *because* of the teacher's light switching technique, or because there were other,

[2]One might even conjecture that the experiments were not only studies of first impressions but were studies of opinions about human behavior. Thus, in the High School Experiment, the students who witnessed the angry-punitive desist rated the teacher as being best able to "control a bunch of tough students," but *not* as being best able to "control students like myself." This may be an experimental demonstration of the prevalence of the *opinion* that the best way to handle tough kids is to be tough.

and perhaps less immediately discernible, managerial techniques that produced a prevailing climate in this classroom that resulted in this technique, *or any other*, being effective? The following day, we observed Teacher B in the same school and same grade also walk to the light switch and flick the lights on and off as a signal for quiet and attention. It didn't work. The children who were talking continued to talk, two boys who were poking each other continued their horseplay, and so on. These are merely single examples. The Videotape research and the High School Interviews and Questionnaires do not deny that some desists are effective and that others are ineffective. These studies do justify the statement that whether a desist is effective or ineffective is *not* dependent upon the qualities of the desist technique as such (except for anger producing discomfort) but rather upon other dimensions of classroom management, related commitments, or prevailing variables.

The research so far has handled half of Josh Billings' statement. We now have learned that we may have "known so many things that ain't so." What have we learned about classroom management that may be shown to be so?

4

WITHITNESS
AND OVERLAPPING

If teachers' desist techniques do not make a difference in how children behave in classrooms, what does? The fact remains that the behavior of the children in the classrooms studied did differ. There was a wide range in scores for work involvement, deviancy, and deviancy contagion. A few classrooms had very high work involvement, most had an average amount of work involvement, and a few had very low work involvement. This was also true for the amount of deviancy and deviancy contagion. What produced these differences? Must we fall back upon the trite, true, but evasive generalization that "it all depends on the teacher and the children?" Or, is it possible to delineate what it is that teachers *do* that makes a difference in how children behave?

An analysis of the first group of videotapes showed that there *were* specific categories of teachers' behavior that correlated with their managerial success as measured by work involvement, deviancy rate, contagion of misbehavior, and effectiveness of desists. Some of the dimensions of teacher behaviors that made a difference in the behavior of pupils were, as we termed them: *withitness* (demonstrating that she knew what was going on); *overlapping* (attending to two issues simultaneously); *transition smoothness* (absence of dangles, flip-flops, and thrusts); and programming for *learning-related variety* in seatwork.

Moreover, the teacher behaviors that were related to managerial success applied to the classroom as a whole and not merely to specific pupils; that is, to those children diagnosed as emotionally disturbed (but not psychotic) as well as to those who were regarded as nondisturbed. There were two findings in support of this conclusion: (1) There were significant positive correlations between the behavior scores of the disturbed and those of the nondisturbed children. These ranged from .57 to .82 dependent upon whether the correlations were obtained between scores for deviancy or scores for work involvement, or between scores in seatwork and scores in recitation settings. (2) Correlations between any teacher style dimension and children's behaviors were in the same direction and approximate magnitude for both the disturbed and nondisturbed children. In other words, whatever the teachers did that was associated with high work involvement and low deviancy for the nondisturbed children was also associated with high work involvement and low deviancy (and deviancy contagion) for the disturbed children.

Except for the effects of programming learning related variety, the correlations between teacher style and pupils' behavior were of the same direction approximate size for the classrooms in Suburb *Y* where grades one and two were videotaped as for Suburb *X* where grades three through five were studied.

There were a few findings that led us to obtain more videotapes of classrooms in order to arrive at more definitive conclusions. These were: (1) Significant differences between children's behavior scores in seatwork and those in recitation; (2) Some differences between the teacher styles associated with managerial success in seatwork and those that were associated with managerial success in recitation. For example, programmed learning related variety was far more important for seatwork than for recitation. (3) One difference between the findings obtained for the first two grades and those obtained for grades 3–5: Learning related variety was significant for the lower elementary grades but not for the upper elementary grades.

Since we videotaped the classrooms for one-half day each we did not obtain data for both seatwork and recitation settings for all teachers. Some teachers did not program both kinds of activities in the one-half day that they were videotaped. Given this reality, in addition to having to discriminate between the lower and upper elementary grades, some correlations were based upon a small number of cases. As a consequence, we expanded the Videotape Study to include more classrooms and to increase the likelihood of obtaining both seatwork and recitation settings for all teachers.

THE SECOND VIDEOTAPE STUDY

The Selection of Classrooms

In the second Videotape Study, fifty first- and second-grade classrooms were videotaped for a full day each. Twenty-four classrooms were located in a predominantly middle-class suburb of Detroit, Mich. and twenty-six were located in Detroit. One classroom from the suburb was eliminated because of technical deficiencies, leaving a final N of forty-nine classrooms.

In order to exclude extreme or atypical classrooms from the study, we used only those Detroit schools where average achievement scores fell between the 20th and 80th percentile of that system's norms. In order to minimize the influence of communities and administrators upon the results and in order to obtain some range of managerial success, we selected schools that were large enough to have at least two classrooms for both grades one and two. We selected those schools that had at least one relatively "poor" and relatively "good" classroom. This difference was based upon the judgment of the principal investigator who visited the classrooms in the fall. This gross judgment was based upon whether the children in the classrooms were rated by him as having high or low degrees of work involvement in academic settings. (The designation of the emotionally disturbed children was based upon a consensus among the teacher, principal, and, in most cases, a school social worker or psychologist.) The classrooms were videotaped in the spring by means of remote-controlled equipment, much as in the initial Videotape Study.

The Scoring of Children's Behavior

An activity map was made for each classroom prior to the coding. This activity map included a description of the activity or activities going on at any particular time, the starting and finishing time of each activity, and the transition points ("All right, will the Brownies put away your arithmetic books and come up to the reading circle.") and transition phases (the time elapsing from the moment the teacher instructed the Brownies to come to the reading circle and their beginning to read) for each activity for each subgroup. The persons mapping the classroom day also made a schematic diagram of the seating arrangement for all the different activities, indicating where the children were at the time, how many were located at each activity session, and also which were boys, girls, or "emotionally disturbed."

The sample of children to be scored was selected by the project director from diagrams of the seating arrangement for each academic setting. The diagram for each setting was divided into four quadrants and one boy and one girl from each quadrant was preselected for scoring. Thus, for each session of particular settings, we attempted to obtain a sampling of the behavior of eight visibly nondisturbed children taken from different geographical locations of the room. This method of selecting precluded selecting children on the basis of any kind of bias—whether because their behavior stood out or whether because they were of interest to the coder for some reason or another. The children designated as emotionally disturbed were scored separately. The final sampling of children used contained more than eight children, since there were different children comprising the recitation subgroups or seatwork subgroups for any one teacher. Thus, the group making up the "Rockets" would be in the reading group at one time while the "Brownies" would be doing seatwork; at another time, the "Brownies" would be at the reading circle while the "Rockets" would be at seatwork.

Each child preselected for scoring was coded for *work involvement* and for *deviancy* every 12 seconds for the duration of the specific academic session. A 12-second interval was used to accommodate the timing device on the videotape playback machine, which cumulatively recorded duration each tenth of a minute.

The *work involvement* was coded by categorizing the behavior of a child as:

1. *Definitely in* the assigned work. To be coded as definitely working, the child had to exhibit overt signs that he was "in" the prescribed activity for most of the 12-second

interval—writing in the prescribed workbook; performing or volunteering to perform in recitation; in a clear posture of attending or reading, etc.

2. *Probably in* the assigned work. For the behavior to be coded in this category, the child had to be in a posture from which it could reasonably be inferred that he was "in" the work (looking at or having proper props before him, oriented physically as though he could be thinking or listening) but not actually writing or otherwise showing clear signs of being "in."

3. *Definitely out* of the assigned work. This was coded when the child showed no actual or postural signs of being "in" or showed clear signs that he was "out" of the prescribed activity–was attending to, or doing something other than the designated task for most of the 12-second interval.

Deviancy was coded by categorizing the behavior of a child for each twelve-second interval as: (1) Not misbehaving; (2) Engaging in mild misbehavior; or (3) engaging in serious misbehavior. Deviant behavior was defined as having: direction and purpose (intentional, and with knowledge that it is deviant), and as being against the teacher, another child, or some reasonably important convention of classroom behavior. It had to have an active behavior quality. This requirement means that a child was not coded as misbehaving just because he may have been criticized by the teacher, unless he had, in fact, knowingly committed a deviant act. Thus, if a teacher reprimanded a child for not sitting up straight, or for mispronouncing a word, the child would not be coded as deviant. (If slouching, however, was an open defiance of an immediate request of the teacher it would be coded as a deviant act: It would have the quality of an intentional act of defiance against the teacher which the child may be assumed to have known was misbehaving.) A *mild deviancy* was one that most teachers in the circumstances would disapprove of, and which they would either ignore or deal with mildly, such as whispering to neighbors during seatwork, making faces at camera, reading a comic book, etc. A *serious deviancy* was an act that most teachers in most classrooms would rarely ignore and would take definite measures to stop. This would be highly intrusive behavior which would interfere with others, would damage property, would lead to potential harm to himself or others, or would violate an important code of a school. Aggressive acts and open defiance of the teacher would generally be coded as serious. (As in the previous Videotape Study, only about 1 percent of the deviancies were coded as serious, and all deviancies were, as a consequence, treated alike statistically.)

The coding of children's behaviors did not start until the designated work for the session had actually begun. Their behavior was not coded while they were making a transition from one activity to another or while they were simply waiting for further instructions. Thus, in a reading recitation, coding of the children's behaviors did not start until the books were distributed and the activity of reading had begun; and coding did not begin for seatwork sessions until the children had accumulated all the necessary props in the proper location and started to work.

The ratios of the intervals coded as "definitely in" to those coded as "definitely out" were averaged to obtain the *work involvement* score for any classroom in seatwork and recitation settings. The *freedom from deviancy* score for any session was the percentage of 12-second intervals in which no misbehavior occurred. (The deviancy rate is thus stated in a positive way for statistical purposes: a low score being a "successful" class.)

The Scoring of Teacher Behavior

In order to avoid coloring teachers' scores with children's behaviors, different coders were assigned to coding the teachers than were used to code the children. The different codes for teachers will be described separately in the related sections of this research report.

WITHITNESS AND OVERLAPPING

The Meaning and Scoring of Withitness

Suppose we are observing desist events. The teacher is conducting a phonics lesson with a group at the reading circle. Johnny, who is in a group that is at seatwork, turns around and whispers to Jimmy. The teacher looks up and says, "Johnny, stop that talking and get busy on your addition problems." This desist was scored for clarity, firmness, child-treatment, and other qualities. These qualities made no difference. Is there anything about this desist event that does relate to managerial success? The videotape was reversed for about a minute and replayed. The coders noticed that two boys, in a different section of the room, were throwing paper airplanes back and forth. This was going on before and during the time the teacher desisted Johnny for talking. Is this fact significant?

Let us observe another desist event. The teacher is teaching addition facts to the entire class as children take turns writing answers to addition problems at the board. Mary leans over toward the table to her right and whispers to Jane. Both she and Jane giggle. The teacher says, "Mary and Jane stop that!" This desist was also scored for various qualities, none of which was found to be significantly related to children's behavior. Again the videotape was reversed and replayed. The observers noted that about forty-five seconds earlier Lucy and John, who were sitting at the same table as Jane, started to whisper. Robert watched this and he too got into the act. Then Jane giggled and said something to John. Then Mary leaned over and whispered to Jane. At this point the teacher desisted Mary and Jane. Is the fact that Mary was a late entry in this talking and giggling chain of any significance?

In the first example, the teacher desisted a minor deviancy (whispering) and did nothing about a more serious deviancy (throwing paper airplanes). In the second example, the deviancy (whispering and giggling) had started sometime earlier and had spread to John, and then to Mary, and then to Jane before the teacher stepped in to stop it.

Do these two events reveal something significant other than the fact that the teacher desisted a misbehavior in a certain manner? We thought we saw some common denominator in these two events. The teacher failed to show that she had "eyes in back of her head." In the first case, she didn't show signs of noticing a more serious deviancy. In the second case, she didn't show signs of noticing a contagion chain building up. Maybe *this* is what is important, and *not* whether she is clear, angry, firm, etc. We called this dimension *withitness* and proceeded to develop a code for this dimension and to replay the videotapes to obtain scores for the teachers that would measure their degree of withitness.

Withitness was defined as a teacher's communicating to the children by her actual behavior (rather than by simple verbal announcing: "I know what's going on.") that she knows what the children are doing, or has the proverbial "eyes in back of her head." What kinds of teacher behaviors, and in what circumstances, provide cues to pupils as to whether the teacher does or does not know what is going on? It is not adequate to measure what a teacher knows in order to obtain a score for the degree of her withitness. It is necessary to measure what she *communicates* she knows. The children, after all, must get the information that she knows or doesn't know what they are doing.

Desist events are examples of incidents where a teacher does something that communicates to the children whether she does or doesn't know what is happening. In such incidents the teacher engages in some overt action that may demonstrate this. In desist events a child is doing something and the teacher does something about it. Does she pick the correct target and does she do it on time? Or, does she make some kind of mistake that communicates the information that she doesn't know what is happening?

In addition to using desist events to obtain measures of desist techniques as such (clarity, firmness, etc.) we also used desist events to obtain measures of withitness. These events satisfy the criteria for a behavioral measure of communicated withitness: (1) a child behavior does occur; (2) a teacher takes some action about this behavior; and (3) the action the teacher takes has the potential of communicating to the children that she does or doesn't know what is going on—that is, she can be correct or make a discernible mistake. In addition, desist events occur with sufficient frequency to provide an adequate sampling. (Other events might also be used to measure withitness, such as a child using an incorrect prop, working problems on the wrong page, etc.) However, actions taken by teachers at these behaviors are not as frequent as desist events. Nor do onlooking children really know whether the teacher is right or wrong, since the event of a child working on the wrong page is not as perceptually clear to onlookers as is the event of a child throwing a paper airplane or making noise.

Each separate and distinguishable desist was categorized as being correct or incorrect for both the *target* of the desist and for its *timing*.

The child or subgroup that the teacher desisted constituted the *target*. The teacher could pick on the correct target or the incorrect target. The target was correct if the teacher desisted the correct deviant or subgroup of deviants (two or more children talking together).

Target mistakes consisted of:

1. The teacher desisted the wrong child for a deviant act, or desisted an onlooker or contagee rather than an initiator.

2. The teacher desisted a less serious deviancy and overlooked a more serious deviancy that was occurring at the time or that had occurred between the time of this desist and the previous one. Thus, if a teacher desisted a child who was whispering to a neighboring child while two children were running around chasing each other, the event would be categorized as a wrong target due to "more serious ignored."

Whether the teacher used correct or incorrect timing was determined by whether or not the deviancy became clearly more serious before the teacher acted. A desist was categorized as correct in timing if the misbehavior was no more serious at the time of the desist than at the time it started. The issue here is not how much time elapsed between the initiation of the deviancy and the teacher's doing something to stop it. Rather, the issue is whether the deviancy increased in seriousness between the time it started and the teacher desisted.

Timing mistakes, or being too late, consisted of:

1. The deviancy *spread* before it was desisted. Thus, if two children started to whisper illegally, then a third joined them, then a fourth joined them and then the teacher desisted for talking, the desist was categorized as being "too late" by reason of its having spread before the teacher stepped in.

2. The deviancy *increased in seriousness* before it was desisted. Thus, if John turned around and whispered to Jim, then Jim poked John, then John poked Jim, then Jim started to pull off John's shirt and John started to pull off Jim's shirt, and then the teacher desisted, the desist was coded as "too late" by reason of having increased in seriousness before the teacher did something about it.

A teacher's withitness score was obtained by dividing the total number of her desists by the number of her mistake-free desists.

The fewer the proportion of the desists that contained either target or timing mistakes, the higher her score for withitness.[1]

The Meaning and Scoring of Overlapping

Let us look at another two desist events. In one, the teacher is working with a reading group and Mary is reading aloud. John and Richard, sitting in the seatwork region, are talking loudly. The teacher looks at John and Richard and at almost the same time says: "Mary, continue reading, I'm listening," then says: "John and Richard I can hear you talk. Now turn around and do your seatwork." In a different desist event, the teacher is also with a reading group and Betty is reading aloud. Gary and Lee, sitting in the seatwork region, are playfully poking each other. The teacher looks up at Gary and Lee, gets up and puts the reading book on her seat, walks over to Gary and Lee, and angrily says: "I want this nonsense stopped! Right now! Lee, you haven't finished your arithmetic problems. Now get to them right now and get them right. And Gary you too!" She then walked back to the reading circle, picked up the reading book, sat down in her chair, and calmly said: "All right, now let's continue with our story."

What qualities are significant about these desist events, if any? It has already been established that differences in the manner of desisting as such, make no difference. What other information might

[1]An attempt was made to code the task withitness of teachers in addition to their behavior withitness. This referred to the degree to which teachers communicated that they were knowledgeable about children's performances in legitimate tasks (reading, arithmetic, etc.) beyond knowing how the child currently reciting or just having completed reciting performed. Mistakes consisted of: incorrect designations of which children performed (saying "Mary read before" when Mary hadn't read before); of what tasks were performed at a previous time (saying "We read about trees this morning" when they hadn't read about trees); of how a child performed previously (saying "Johnny didn't finish his arithmetic" when Johnny did finish his arithmetic); or making mistakes about subject matter content. The vast majority of the teachers made no task related mistakes, and the few teachers who did made, at most, two such mistakes. Task related withitness may or may not be correlated with managerial success. However, the question cannot be answered since, in reality, the occurrence of task related mistakes by elementary school teachers is so rare, and differences among teachers in this respect so minimal, that the hypothesis cannot even be tested with our data.

we derive from these events? After studying many desist events we noticed that there are times when teachers become completely immersed in the deviancy issue and drop the ongoing activity—they go "all out" to handle the deviancy and do nothing about the activity they are deflected from. This happened in the example involving Gary and Lee. In this incident, the teacher put the reading book down, physically removed herself from the reading group, changed her emotional tone, and became immersed in handling Gary and Lee. She didn't even glance at the reading group during this episode.

There are also desist events when the teacher, in some manner, attends to both the deviancy and the ongoing task. This was the case in the desist involving John and Richard. In this episode, the teacher maintained the same emotional tone, remained seated with the reading group, and issued a statement to the reading group almost simultaneously with her beginning to desist John and Richard. In this incident she showed signs of attending to both the reading group and to the deviancy. Is *this* the quality that is important? Does what a teacher does when she has two issues to confront at one time make any difference in her managerial success?

Are there any other events in a classroom that have this double-issue property? Let us look at two child intrusion events. In one, the teacher is at the reading circle and Lucy is reading aloud while standing. Johnny, who was doing seatwork at his desk, walks up toward the teacher holding his workbook. The teacher glances at Johnny, then looks back at Lucy, nodding at Lucy, as Lucy continues to read aloud. The teacher remains seated and takes Johnny's workbook. She placed a check next to an answer in Johnny's book as she looked at Johnny. She turned to Lucy saying, "That was a hard word, Lucy, and you pronounced it right." She checked about three more answers in Johnny's book, saying: "That's fine, you can go ahead and do the next page now," and resumed looking at the reading book as Lucy continued reading.

Let us look at another child intrusion episode. In this one, the teacher is seated in front of a reading circle while Suzanne is reading aloud while standing. Mary walks up from the seatwork group holding a workbook and stands next to the teacher. The teacher continues to look at her reading book while Suzanne reads. After about fifteen seconds, Mary tugs at the teacher's sleeve. The teacher gets up from her seat, puts the reading book down, and checks the problem in Mary's workbook for about thirty seconds. She then turns to the next page and points out further work for Mary to do. (Suzanne, in the meantime, stopped reading aloud and watched the teacher.) The teacher then picks up the reading book, sits down, and says: "O.K. Suzanne, suppose you continue reading."

There is nothing spectacular about these events. But is there something about teacher style that they reveal and that might bear some relationship to managerial success? They are both two-issue events: there is an ongoing activity the teacher is involved in and there is a child bring-in that intrudes into the ongoing activity. In the first example, the teacher attended to both the reading activity and the child intrusion almost simultaneously. In the second, she completely withdrew her attention from Suzanne in the reading group, became totally immersed in Mary, and then resumed her attention to Suzanne.

It seemed to us that the desist events and the child intrusion events had a common denominator. They both presented a teacher with two issues at one time. We called these overlapping situations. And we proceeded to ask a simple question about the overlapping situations: Do teachers attend to both or do they become immersed in one to the exclusion of the other? And, if there are differences in teacher styles in this respect, do these differences relate to managerial success? In order to answer these questions we developed a code and replayed the videotapes to score all desist events and child intrusion events for teachers' overlappingness.

Overlapping refers to what the teacher does when she has two matters to deal with at the same time. Does she somehow attend to both issues simultaneously or does she remain or become immersed in one issue only, to the neglect of the other? These kinds of "overlapping" issues occur in both desist events and in child intrusion events.

An overlapping issue is present at the time of a desist event when the teacher is occupied with an ongoing task with children at the time that she desists a deviancy. Thus, if she is in a recitation setting with a reading group and she notes and acts upon a deviancy occurring in the seatwork setting, she is in an overlapping situation. Overlapping may also occur when the teacher is involved in a recitation setting and the desist occurs in the recitation setting. At this time she is confronted with two issues: one is the ongoing recitation activity she is involved with and the other is the deviancy she is desisting.

A desist event is not an overlapping situation when the teacher is "open" or already engaged in desisting. If she is walking around the room supervising seatwork, or sitting at her desk, then she is "open." She is not at that time engaged in an ongoing task with a group or subgroup of children. If she desists at such open times she has but one management issue to handle and that issue is the deviancy. Similarly, if she is engaged in a chain desist or is already desisting ("John, keep quiet," then "and Mary, you be quiet too," and "Jim, sit down") all in one sequence uninterrupted by engaging in some task related behavior then a desist occurring within this sequence is not an overlapping situation. For, in these circumstances, there is only one issue and that is the one of deviancy management. There is no other issue the teacher is engaged with at the time. Such one-issue desists are, therefore, not considered as events during which overlapping is to be coded.

An overlapping issue is also present during child intrusions and child "bring ins" when these occur at the time the teacher is engaged in some activity with a subgroup of children. Thus, if a child from the seatwork setting approaches the teacher with a paper in hand to show her while the teacher is working with a reading group, this event constitutes an overlapping situation. At this time, the teacher has two issues to deal with: the ongoing reading task and the child with the "bring in." As was the case with desist events, if the teacher was open at the time of the child intrusion event, then this was the only issue present at the time. Such one-issue child intrusion events were not coded for overlapping.

The code for overlapping was designed to answer one question: When the teacher is confronted with two issues simultaneously does she attend to both during the event or does she not? In this code, we were not concerned with coding how she handled the issues, or with whether she handled them successfully or unsuccessfully, or wisely or unwisely, but merely with whether she manifested some act that evidenced her *paying attention* to both issues or to only one of either of the two issues. The act of "attention to" might be a remark, a direction, or a simple look.

The code for overlapping, for both desist events and child intrusion events, consisted of two categories,[2] some overlapping and no overlapping.

Some overlapping was indicated when the teacher evidenced some act of attending to both issues during the event. Example: The teacher was listening to John read when Mary (from seatwork group) walked up to the teacher and stood next to her holding a paper in her hand. The teacher glanced at Mary, continued to listen to John's reading for about five seconds, then told Mary to "wait a minute," and resumed listening to John. The teacher may have told Mary to get back to her seat, or merely have held up her hand or a finger in a gesture signalling a wait to Mary, for this event to have been categorized as showing some overlapping. As an example: The teacher was listening to Mary read in the reading group, then looked at two boys in the arithmetic seatwork group who were making paper airplanes. *She turned back to Mary, saying*: "*Keep on reading.*" Then she got up, walked toward the two boys . . . Or, the teacher may have simply *looked back* at the reading group after walking towards the two boys in order to have categorized the event as having some overlapping. Any overt act, no matter how short or mild, manifesting *some* attention to both issues was adequate to code an overlapping event as showing some overlap on the part of the teacher.

No overlapping was coded when the teacher manifested no attention to either one of the two overlapping issues. She either remained "glued" to the initial ongoing activity without any manifestation of attention to the child intrusion beyond the minimum necessary to know it was there; or she dropped the ongoing activity entirely and became totally immersed in the intrusion or deviancy issue. Signs of "total immersion" in the intrusion or deviancy were: physical movement away from the ongoing activity to the region where the deviancy was occurring; change in manner and affect (from quiet to loud, friendly to angry); staying with the deviancy for longer than necessary with "nagging"

[2]In the initial Videotape Study, six categories of degrees of overlapping were reliably discriminated, but these were collapsed into "some" or "none" in the statistical analysis. Consequently, we only used these two categories when coding the second Videotape Study.

and "overtalking" about and to the deviants; and similar behaviors indicating total going out and immersion in the deviancy, concurrent with total leaving of the ongoing activity without any overt sign of attention to the latter.

Results Relating to Overlapping, Withitness, and Managerial Success

The product-moment correlations between the measures of teacher style and the measures of managerial success (deviancy and work involvement) for both recitation and seatwork settings are presented in Appendix 4.1. The results of intercorrelating the various measures of teacher style are presented in Appendix 4.2.

The results show that both withitness and overlapping are significantly related to managerial success. In recitation settings, the correlation of withitness is .615 with work involvement and .531 with freedom from deviancy rate. In seatwork settings, withitness correlates .307 with work involvement and .509 with freedom from deviancy rate. Withitness, then, may be said to induce work involvement, especially in recitation settings, and to restrain deviancy in both recitation and seatwork settings.

Overlapping correlates .460 with work involvement and .362 with freedom from deviancy in recitation settings. In seatwork settings, overlapping correlates .379 with freedom from deviancy and .259 with work involvement (which is not quite statistically significant). Overlapping, then, does discourage deviancy in both recitation and seatwork settings but relates to work involvement in recitation settings only.

These correlational analyses do tell us that both withitness and overlapping are associated with managerial success. Of the two, withitness appears to be more important, in the sense of being more highly correlated with children's behavior. (This was also true in the initial videotape study.) These two aspects of teacher style also correlate with each other, which means that the teachers who manifest more withitness also tend to be the teachers who show more signs of actively attending to two issues simultaneously when two issues are concurrently present. (This was also true in the initial videotape study.) This gives rise to some additional questions. Would withitness be associated with managerial success if it weren't tied up with overlapping? Would overlapping be related to managerial success if it weren't correlated with withitness? Could either of these dimensions of teacher style stand on its own feet and relate to managerial success without being bound up with the other?

The meaning of this question might be clarified by a hypothetical example. Suppose we found a correlation between football players' height and their percentage of successful tackles: Taller football players had higher percentages of successful tackles. Suppose this was also true for weight—that heavier players had more successful tackles than lighter players. Suppose, however, height and weight were correlated and tall players tended to be heavier than short players. Would height alone, or would weight alone, relate to the degree of successful tackles? There is a statistical technique that enables one to cancel out the effects of height to see whether weight alone relates to successful tackles. Or, one could partial out the effects of weight to see whether height by itself correlated with the percentage of successful tackles. In essence, one would arbitrarily assign all players the same height and then see whether differences in weight correlated with successful tackles, or assign all players the same weight to see whether height alone correlates with successful tackles. The statistical technique involved is called partial correlation—it partials out or cancels out the effects of one variable from another.

Such partial correlational analyses were made for the various teacher dimensions measured in this research. These are presented in Appendix 4.3 through Appendix 4.6.

What is the answer to the hypothetical question of whether withitness and overlapping could operate alone? If one partials out the effects of overlapping from withitness what does this do to the correlations between withitness and managerial success? Or, if one removes the effects of withitness from overlapping what does this do to the correlations between overlapping and managerial success?

In general, an analysis of the results by means of partial correlations indicates that withitness by itself has more relationship with managerial success than does overlapping by itself. The correlation of .615 between work involvement and withitness in recitation settings is reduced to .477 (still significant) when the effect of overlapping is removed. In contrast, the correlation of .460 between overlapping and work involvement in recitation settings becomes insignificant (.146) when the contribution of withitness is removed. For freedom from deviancy in recitation settings, the correlation with withitness is still significant (.422) when the effect of overlapping is removed; however, the correlation with overlapping becomes insignificant (.065) when the effect of withitness is removed. Similar results obtain for the relative impact of withitness and overlapping upon freedom from deviancy in seatwork: the correlation with withitness remains significant (.380) even after removing the effects of overlapping whereas the correlation with overlapping becomes insignificant (.107) after removing the effects of withitness.

Considering the results of both Videotape Studies, one may conclude that both the withitness and the overlapping of teachers have a significant bearing upon their managerial success but that the effects of withitness are greater than the effects of overlapping. Throughout, the correlations of withitness with both work involvement and freedom from deviancy scores are higher than the correlations between teachers' overlapping scores and children's behavior. Moreover, the correlations between withitness and managerial success remain significant even after the removal of the effects of overlapping, while the correlations between overlapping and managerial success become insignificant after the removal of the effects of withitness.

Both Videotape Studies, however, show that overlapping and withitness are significantly related to each other. To reiterate, teachers who show signs of attending to more than one issue when there is more than one issue to handle at a particular time, are likely to pick correct deviancy targets and do something about the deviancy on time—before the deviancy becomes more serious or begins to spread to other children. On the other hand, teachers who become immersed in one issue only when there is more than one issue to handle, are more likely to act upon an incorrect deviancy target or act upon the deviancy too late—after the misbehavior becomes more serious or spreads to other children. And handling the *correct* deviant *on time* is evidently more important than *the method* used in handling the deviancy.[3]

[3]The reader may or may not wish to extrapolate this generalization to the management of delinquency on streets.

How might one interpret the relationship between withitness and overlapping? One interpretation is that broadening one's scope of active attending, as manifest in overlapping, *enables* a teacher to receive more information about what is going on. This knowledge is necessary to achieve withitness. However, overlapping is not adequate unless it leads to some behavior that communicates to the children. Children probably do not categorize an overlapping dimension or even perceive it. What they do see, categorize in some way, and react to, is what the teacher *does*. They do see her pick on the wrong person or do it too late, in which case they form a judgment, however explicit or implicit, that she doesn't know what is going on. However, if she acts promptly and on the correct deviant than they see her as having "eyes in the back of her head." And, if the children perceive her as knowing what is going on she is more likely to induce worklike behavior and restrain deviancy than if they see her as not knowing what is going on. Thus, overlapping correlates with withitness (enables withitness to occur) but does not, in and of itself, relate to managerial success, whereas withitness does. Regardless of the type of theoretical linkage between overlapping and withitness, the reality of classrooms dictates that both relate to managerial success and, unless some other technique is available to obtain knowledge about what is going on except by attending, one can safely recommend that teachers engage in both manifest overlapping and demonstrated withitness.

5

MOVEMENT MANAGEMENT: SMOOTHNESS AND MOMENTUM

THE ISSUE OF MOVEMENT MANAGEMENT

The classrooms that were on videotapes contained an average of 33.2 major changes in learning activities involving either the entire class or official subgroups of the class. This count was based on transitions into major academic activities such as arithmetic, or semi-academic activities such as drawing. This count did not include transitions into nonacademic activities such as recess, or administrative activities such as collecting milk money.

A teacher in a self-contained classroom, then, must manage considerable activity *movement:* she must initiate, sustain, and terminate many activities. Sometimes this involves having children move physically from one point of the room to another, as when a group must move from their own desks to the reading circle. At other times it involves some psychological movement, or some change in props, as when children change from doing arithmetic problems at their desks to studying spelling words at the same desks.

How do teachers go about initiating and maintaining activity-flow in a classroom? Are there sizeable differences among teachers in this respect, and, if so, do these differences relate to differences in the amount of work-involvement or deviancy of children? Is it possible to delineate concrete behaviors of teachers that one can use to constitute measures of movement management?

Or, must one resort to impressionistic judgments or ratings having to do with "smoothness," "jerkiness," "dragginess," or "really moving"?

Let us look at two simple transitions to see whether they provide some suggestion as to the kinds of teacher behaviors that might be used to specify some aspects of movement management.

Miss Smith is with the Rocket subgroup at the reading circle while the other subgroups are at their desks doing seatwork. Mary has just finished reading. The teacher says: "That's fine, Mary. And that finishes the story. Now return to your desks and finish your seatwork." The teacher closes the book and then looks around the room for about three seconds. She then says: "All right, the Bluebirds can come to the reading circle now."

Miss Jones is with the Brownies at the reading circle while the other subgroups are doing seatwork at their desks. John has just finished reading. The teacher closes her book and says: "That's good, John. Now all of you get back to your desks and finish your seatwork." She immediately says: "Cubs, it's your turn to come to the reading circle now."

These are two ordinary transitions. There is nothing spectacular, dramatic, or very different about either one. In both, the teacher is simply changing the subgroups at the reading circle. Since we were looking for aspects of movement management we noted one difference. Miss Smith paused and looked around the classroom for about three seconds before calling the second group to the reading circle. Miss Jones did not pause or scan the room before calling the second group to the reading circle. One might say that Miss Smith "wasted" a few seconds by looking around before calling on the next group. On the other hand, Miss Jones issued her direction suddenly and did nothing to see what the Cubs were doing before issuing her order. We called the latter a *thrust*, and saw it as jarring and jerky. Does the prevalence of this kind of jerkiness in a teacher's style make any difference in how children behave? Is it "good" because it may save time, or is it "bad" because it may produce jerkiness? Or doesn't it make any difference?

Let us look at another example of an aspect of movement management. The teacher is reviewing arithmetic problems with the entire class. Richard just finished giving the answer to the last problem in the work book. The teacher says: "That's correct,

Richard." The teacher closes her copy of the arithmetic work book and says: "All right, lets put away the arithmetic and take out your readers." After the children proceeded to do this she says: "Let's see now. How many got all the problems right?. . . .That's very good; most of you got them all correct. All right, now let's get at our readers." At this point, being concerned with movement management, we ignored the issue of eliciting feedback and of complimenting performances, and looked at the simple issue of the teacher's sequencing: her stopping the arithmetic lesson, starting the lesson in the reader, and then going back to the arithmetic. Does this kind of *flip-flopping* produce any significant interference with smoothness of movement and does it have any impact upon children's behavior?

Not all teachers' behaviors relating to the dimension of smoothness-jerkiness occur at transition points. A teacher may conduct an ongoing recitation with varying degrees of smoothness or of jerkiness. For example: The teacher is conducting a lesson in oral reading. All the children have their story books in front of them. The teacher is in front of the class and Suzanne just finished reading a portion of the story. The teacher says: "All right, that's fine. Mary, will you continue reading." Mary stands up and begins to read. While listening to Mary, the teacher happens to glance down an aisle, and walks toward a girl's desk, saying: "What is this doing on the floor?" The teacher then picks up a paper bag that was lying on the floor, saying: "What is your lunch bag doing here? You know you're supposed to keep your lunch bag in the cloak room. Now put it away." The teacher inspectingly looks up and down the aisles, then starts to walk back toward the front of the class to resume listening to Mary read.

This example of a teacher's becoming deflected from the main activity by reacting to an unobtrusive bag might exemplify another kind of jerkiness. This was labeled *stimulus-boundedness*. Do these stimulus-bound behaviors on the part of teachers belong in the category of smoothness-jerkiness and, if so, do they detract from work-involvement and encourage deviancy? Or, do they serve to transmit the teacher's concern with order and rules and thus discourage deviancy and promote work-involvement? Or, do they make no difference?

Since the management of movement is one of the tasks of a classroom teacher, we decided to investigate its relationship to the behavior of children. The smoothness-jerkiness part of movement was measured by identifying five kinds of teachers' behaviors related to this dimension. These were: stimulus-bound episodes, thrusts, flip-flops, dangles, and truncations. These categories and the behaviors comprising them will be elaborated in the next section of this chapter.

Another aspect of activity movement concerns the rate of flow, or momentum. Is momentum sustained? Do activities keep moving in an appropriate pace? Or, are activities slowed down, held back, and made to appear draggy? More importantly, what is it that teachers *do* to keep activities moving forward or to hold them back?

Let us look at an example of one type of slowdown. The teacher is starting a lesson about telling time and is walking toward the blackboard, saying: "I have some times on the board I would like for you to designate on the clocks that you're going to make yourself." Margaret groaned softly. The teacher turned to Margaret and *slowly* said: "Now, Margaret, did you come to school to learn?" The teacher paused for about three seconds, looking at Margaret. "Is it so painful, Margaret?" Another pause. "No, I don't think so. Your parents are going to want you to tell time." Pause. "And you're going to be very happy to learn telling time, Margaret. You don't have to make all those groans because you don't want to tell time. But, after all, if your mother sees you can tell time you might get a watch of your own." The teacher then turned to the whole class, saying: "Let us all sit up tall," and resumed the lesson.

One might assume that the teacher lectured Margaret in order to discourage groaning and to motivate Margaret to learn how to tell time. Is this what it accomplished? Or, does this kind of nagging or *over dwelling* upon behavior produce a slowdown in the activity movement, reduce work-involvement, and increase misbehavior?

Suppose we look at another type of prevalent incident. The teacher is directing the Thunderbird group to come to the reading circle from their desks. She says: "All right, it's the Thunderbirds' turn to come up to the reading circle. John Jones, will you stand up, please?" John stands up. "Now, John, you walk carefully to that seat." John does this. "Now, Mary, you get up and take the seat over there." Mary gets up and walks to the seat at the reading circle. "Richard, it's your turn now." Richard walks up. The teacher then turns to Margaret and directs her to the reading circle. This continues until all ten children comprising the Thunderbirds are seated at the reading circle, and then the teacher sits in front of the group and starts the reading lesson.

One might suppose that the teacher had each child in the Thunderbird group go to the reading circle singly in order to have more control and create more order. Does this technique accomplish this purpose? It can also be seen as a type of slowdown, which was named *group fragmentation*. As a technique that slows down momentum, does it result in more deviancy and less work-involvement?

There was a variety of types of slowdowns in addition to group fragmentation and overdwelling upon behavior. All possessed the common element of teachers' engaging in behaviors that impeded the momentum of the activity. These will be defined in the third section of this chapter. The question is whether the maintenance of momentum, as another aspect of management, has a significant bearing upon the behavior of children.

A reader will probably notice that the following movement codes consist of mistakes made by teachers in the management of movement. There is a reason for this delineation of mistakes. It is easier to notice and categorize those behaviors of teachers that are disruptive of activity movement than it is to denote concrete behaviors that are conducive to effective movement. There is very little to "score" about a teacher when activity is "really moving" and is going smoothly.

When a successful teacher tells the arithmetic seatwork group to come to the reading circle and the reading group to return to their seats and work on their arithmetic books, the children conform quickly and without any deviancy. The traffic moves. Both groups of children get their supplies, get to the proper location, get with the designated activities, and behave appropriately after they're in. To an observer, a successful teacher makes the management of a classroom look easy and makes it appear as though she "isn't doing anything." There is much more for an observer to notice (and score) for both children and teachers in poorly managed classrooms.

An analogy may serve to clarify this point. There is relatively little that can be said about the actions of excellent violinists or basketball players compared to what can be said about the actions of poor violinists or basketball players. To an observer, the performances of the excellent players appear smooth and easy, and there are very few concrete acts that the observer can delineate when describing these excellent performances. There is much more than can be described about a poor performance. The poor basketball player makes observable mistakes than can be categorized and counted: misses shots, misses throws, passes too long or too short for a receiver, stumbles, and so on; the poor violinist plays a sharp instead of a flat, plays an upbow instead of a downbow, starts a note too soon or too late, moves his bow before or after he moves his fingers, and so on. If one were to try to obtain scores for violinists' performances it would be easier to count discernible mistakes than to count all the possible correct things they do. Similarly, it is easier to code mistakes that teachers make in movement management than to code all the possible things they do correctly.

The following teacher codes, then, consist of observable mistakes made in managing activity movement. Two categories of movement mistakes are: (a) behaviors producing *jerkiness*. These are actions of teachers that interfere with the smoothness of the flow of activities; and (b) behaviors producing *slowdowns*. These are behaviors of teachers that impede the momentum of activities. The codes follow.

THE MEASUREMENT OF JERKINESS (ANTI-SMOOTHNESS)

The jerkiness code delineates various behaviors initiated by teachers that interfere with the smoothness of movement in academic activities. This code includes perceptible actions *initiated by* a teacher which produce stops or jarring breaks in the activity flow. These may be short, momentary jerks or relatively long episodes. Events which are not initiated by the teacher and to which she reacts that interrupt the smoothness of an activity such as those caused by fire engine sirens, a sick child, principal's messages, most deviancies, nondeliberate coughs, and the like, are not coded for teacher style. The categories comprising the jerkiness code are discussed in the following paragraphs.

Stimulus-Boundedness

Stimulus-boundedness may be contrasted with goal-directedness. Does the teacher maintain a focus upon an activity goal or is she easily deflected from it? In a stimulus-bound event, a teacher behaves as though she has no will of her own and reacts to some unplanned and irrelevant stimulus as an iron filing reacts to a magnet: She gets magnetized and lured into reacting to some minutia that pulls her out of the main activity stream. The conditions for coding a stimulus-bound event occur when the teacher is engaged in some ongoing activity with a group of children, happens to become aware of some stimulus or event that is minor and unrelated to the ongoing activity, becomes distracted by this stimulus, and reacts to it with sufficient involvement to warrant judging that she is immersed in it to the point of dropping her focus on the ongoing activity. To be coded as a stimulus-bound event the following characteristics must be present: (1) The teacher is engaged in an activity with a group of children—she is *not* open; (2) A stimulus (a child behavior or an object) just "pops into" the teacher's field of attention (i.e., the teacher just happens to walk by it, see, or hear it); (3) The stimulus is not intrusive or intense; (4) The teacher reacts to the event in such a manner as to warrant saying it *pulls her to it* much as a magnet pulls an iron filing to its field; and (5) The teacher must get *into*, or immersed in the stimulus-induced event, and deflected from the ongoing activity for a noticeable amount of time. (A side comment would be insufficient to warrant coding an event as stimulus-bound.)

Some examples of stimulus-bound events are: (1) The teacher was explaining a workbook assignment as the children were concurrently writing answers in their workbooks. She was slowly walking down a row, looking at children's work as she was explaining the problem. She happened to look on the floor and suddenly said: "What's that piece of paper doing on the floor? Who put it there? Jimmy, pick it up please." After looking around the entire floor she resumed explaining the seatwork assignment. (2) The teacher was explaining an arithmetic problem as the children were working along with her in their workbooks. She looked up from the board and suddenly walked about six steps to Jimmy (who was leaning on his left elbow while working the answer) and said: "Jimmy, sit up straight. How can you pay attention and write well when you're slouching like that? Now sit up real straight." She "guidingly" got him to sit erect, saying: "There, that's better." She then walked back to the front of the room and began working the next problem with the class. (3) The teacher was conducting a recitation with a subgroup. She was walking towards a child who was reciting when she passed by the fish bowl. She suddenly stopped walking toward the boy, and stopped at the fish bowl, saying: "Oh my, I forgot to feed the fish!" She then got some fish food from a nearby shelf and started to feed the fish, saying: "My, see how hungry it is." She then turned to a girl, saying: "See, Margaret, you forgot to feed the fish. You can see how hungry it is. See how quickly it comes up to eat."

These examples contained the requirements for stimulus-bound events:

1. The teacher was not open and was engaged in an activity with children.
2. The teacher just "happened" to notice the paper on the floor, the boy slouching, or the fish bowl.
3. The stimulus was not intrusive or interfering in any noticeable way.
4. The stimulus started the teacher's reaction—the teacher did not initiate it or plan it.
5. The teacher got *into* the event, to the degree that an observer who was describing the occurrence would identify this as a meaningful unit of the teacher's behavior, i.e., "she was telling the children to pick up papers," "she was getting Jimmy to sit up straight," "she was feeding the fish."

Minor deviancies might also be coded as stimulus-bound events, dependent upon the manner in which a desist got started, what the teacher was doing just prior to desisting, and whether the teacher got out of the ongoing activity and into the desisting—(was "helplessly" deflected from her goal at the time).

Thrusts

A thrust consists of a teacher's sudden "bursting in" on the children's activities with an order, statement, or question in such a manner as to indicate that her own intent or desire was the only determinant of her timing and point of entry. That is, she evidenced no sign (pausing, looking around) of looking for, or of being sensitive to, the group's readiness to receive her message. A thrust has a clear element of suddenness as well as an absence of any observable sign of awareness or sensitivity to whether the target-audience is in a state of readiness. An everyday example of a thrust would be someone's "butting in" on a conversation of two or more people without waiting to be noticed or attempting to "ease in" by listening to find out what was being discussed. A thrust is the equivalent (in the sense of jerkiness) of a stimulus-bound event except that in stimulus-boundedness the event is started by a stimulus outside of the teacher, whereas in a thrust the event is initiated by an intent of the teacher.

Thrusts can occur at transition points. An example: The teacher is at the reading circle with the Table-1 group. John just finished his turn reading aloud. The teacher quickly closed her book and, without pausing or looking up, said loudly, "Table-2, it's your turn now to come to the reading circle."

Thrusts can also occur during an ongoing recitation. An example: The Eagles were sitting around the reading circle. In preparation for a story about shopping, the children were taking turns discussing their shopping experiences. The teacher was leaning forward, facing Mary, who was telling about going to the supermarket with her mother. As soon as Mary finished, three children raised their hands to volunteer. The teacher suddenly turned around, faced the blackboard, and without looking around at the rest of the children or saying anything to Mary, said, "Look at the board. There are some new words that will be in the next story. Jimmy, read the first one."

Dangles

A dangle was coded when a teacher started, or was in, some activity and then left it "hanging in midair" by going off to some other activity. Following such a "fade away" she would then resume the activity.

Dangles could occur at transition points. An example: The Rockets just completed reading a story at the reading circle. The teacher then got up and started walking to the blackboard, saying, "Now, let's look at these arithmetic problems over there on the blackboard." Halfway to the blackboard she stopped, turned around, walked to her desk and started to look at some papers there. After ten seconds at her desk, she returned to the problems on the blackboard.

Dangles could also occur during an ongoing recitation. An example: The teacher is engaged in checking the children's previous seatwork. Children are taking turns reading their answers to the arithmetic problems. The teacher said "that's right" after Jimmy finished reading his answer to the third problem. She then looked around and said, "All right, Mary, read your answer to the fourth problem." As Mary was getting up, the teacher looked around the room, and said, "My now. Let's see. Suzanne isn't here, is she? Does anyone know why Suzanne is absent today?"

Truncations

A truncation is the same as a dangle, except that in a truncation the teacher does not resume the initiated, then dropped, activity. One might say that a truncation is a longer-lasting dangle.

Flip-flops

Flip-flops were coded only at transition points. A transition entails terminating one activity (put away spelling papers) and starting another (take out your workbooks and turn to page 190). In a flip-flop a teacher terminates one activity, starts another, and then initiates a return to the activity that she had terminated. An example: The teacher says, "All right, let's everybody put away your spelling papers and take out your arithmetic books." The children put their spelling papers in their desks, and, after most of the children had their arithmetic books out on their desks, the teacher asked, "Let's see the hands of the ones who got all their spelling words right."

A teacher's score for smoothness consisted of one minus the total number of jerkiness incidents divided by the number of 6-second units coded. (The number of units coded is equivalent to the total time. This dividend was subtracted from one in order to rank the teachers on the basis of a hypothesized positive smoothness—so that high scores would be regarded as "good" and low scores as "bad.")

THE MEANING AND MEASUREMENT OF SLOWDOWNS

Slowdowns consisted of those behaviors initiated by teachers that clearly slowed down the rate of movement in a recitation activity. Slowdowns refer to movement properties that may or may not be both smooth and unidirectional but which clearly impede or produce friction in the forward momentum of an activity. Their effect is to hold back and produce dragginess in the progress of an activity.

Two categories of slowdowns were coded: overdwelling and fragmentation. The content of this code follows.

Overdwelling

Overdwelling was coded when the teacher dwelled on an issue and engaged in a stream of actions or talk that was clearly beyond what was necessary for most children's understanding or getting with an activity. Overdwelling would produce a reaction on the part of most children of: "All right, all right, that's enough already!" Overdwelling could apply to either the behavior of children or to the task. Following are the categories of overdwelling utilized in this code:

1. *Behavior overdwelling ("Nags")* refers to behaviors of teachers that were focused upon how the children were behaving. This category of overdwelling could generally be characterized as "nagging" or "preaching," and consisted of overdwelling upon misbehavior beyond what was adequate to get a misbehavior stopped or to produce conformity.

Example: The teacher looked up at Richard and said: "Richard, stop that talking." Following this, she changed her focus from Richard and started to talk to the entire class. "Some of you are cooperating and some of you aren't. Mary is cooperating and doing her work and so is Jimmy. Mabel was not listening. Now you all know this is not a playground. This is a classroom and we're supposed to be learning. Good citizens don't bother other children who are trying to learn, do they? So let's all cooperate and be good citizens and not disturb other children. You know it's hard to learn when there's a lot of noise." This incident was categorized as behavior overdwelling because it would slow down the activity movement if the children listened to the teacher, and the coder presumed the children already knew the content—that it was a classroom, etc. The teacher's preachments, then, were not clarifications but were more in the line of nagging.

2. *Actone overdwelling* consists of concentrating on a sub-part of a more inclusive behavior unit. Thus, "holding a fork" is a sub-part of the more inclusive behavior unit of "eating." Similarly, "holding pencil," "reading problem," "writing answer on the paper," are sub-parts of the behavior unit called "doing an arithmetic problem." Actone overdwelling was coded when a teacher focused more on actones than upon the task to the degree that would detract from getting on with the major task. Thus, a teacher would dwell upon how to hold a pencil, where to put a book, how to sit, how and where to stand, where to face. Example: while starting an arithmetic lesson a teacher lectured, "I see some children slouching. John, Mary. I just don't see how you can think well if you sit like you're lazy or half asleep. Now sit up straight. Everybody, let's sit up real straight like you're wide awake and have your thinking caps on. I like the way Suzanne is sitting. And Harold. . ." An example during recitation: The children were at the reading circle taking turns reading. While Mary was reading the teacher stopped her and said: "Now Mary, you can do better than that. Hold your head up and face the other children. That's better. Now stand up straight like you're not afraid. Put your chest out and hold your book away from your face. Like this." Teacher got up and extended Mary's arms so that Mary's book was farther from her face. The teacher then turned toward the remainder of the reading group, saying: "And you can be better listeners. Let's all sit up straight too. John, you can sit up taller. So can you, Jimmy. All right, I guess we're all ready, so Mary continue reading."

3. *Prop overdwelling* was coded when the teacher overemphasized the props (pencils, books, paper, crayons) used in an activity to the point of temporarily losing the focus on the activity. Prop overdwelling need not be accompanied by talk. Thus, a teacher may overemphasize props by her manner—by slowly, almost "caressingly," passing out mimeographed sheets of paper one at a

time to one child at a time, clearly dragging out this procedure and producing significant waiting, to the point of focusing more of the children's attention upon the props than upon the task for which they are to be used.

Example: The teacher is just starting a reading group at the reading circle while the rest of the children are engaged in seatwork with workbooks. She sat in front of the reading group and asked, "All right, who can tell me the name of our next chapter?" Before a child was called on to answer, she looked toward the children at seatwork, saying: "Let's wait until the people in Group Two are settled and working." (Actually, most are writing in their workbooks.) She then looked at John who was in the seatwork group, naggingly asking, "Did you find your pencil?" John answered something which was inaudible. The teacher got up from her seat, saying, "I'd like to know what you did with it." Pause for about two seconds. "Did you eat it?" Another pause. "What happened to it? What color was it? You can't do your work without it." The teacher then went to her desk to get a pencil to give to John, saying, "I'll get you a pencil. Make sure the pencil is here tomorrow morning. And don't tell me you lost that one too. And make it a new one, and see that it's sharpened." The teacher then returned to the reading circle. This pencil transaction lasted 1.4 minutes.

4. *Task overdwelling* is the same as behavior overdwelling but as applied to the task rather than to the behavior of children. In task overdwelling, the teacher overelaborates explanations and directions beyond what would be required for most children to understand, to the point where most children would actually be held back from progressing with the task if they were to be listening to her.

Example: The teacher was explaining adding by twos to the children in preparation for their selecting answers in their workbooks for a seatwork assignment. She walked to a large chart which had all the numbers from one through 100 listed consecutively. In a unison fashion she had the children call out with her while she was pointing and simultaneously naming the odd numbers: "One, three, five, seven, nine, eleven, thirteen, fifteen, seventeen," and on through ninety-nine.

Example: The children are practicing handwriting and most of them are writing. The teacher is walking around saying, "Remember your 'O's' are round. And we do not write small. Remember to put your fingers down for spacing." The teacher then walks to Robert, talking so all can hear: "You were not listening. How does that look to you?" Pause. "Are you in such a hurry this morning? Well, you slow down and wait for us. Read it carefully." Pause. "Your letters are not high enough. Mrs. Wellman has been talking about that for the last month. You start out high. You start slowing down. You're making your letters so small I need a magnifying glass to read them. You have to make it large enough so that other people can read it and enjoy what you're writing." The teacher walks to the front of the room, and in the same tone of voice starts to talk to the total class, saying, "It's not how fast you write, it's how well you do it. Take your time. Make sure that your letters are made right. That looks much better, William." She walks toward William's seat, continuing with, "William is taking his time. I can tell by the way he's writing." This talk consumed 1.5 minutes.

Fragmentation

The other type of slowdown consisted of frangmentation. A fragmentation is a slowdown produced by a teacher's breaking down an activity into sub-parts when the activity could be performed as a single unit. The sub-parts could be single members of a larger group of children (group fragmentation) or sub-actions of a more inclusive behavior unit (prop or actone). The two categories of fragmentation coded were:

1. *Group fragmentation* was coded whenever a teacher had single members of a group do something singly and separately what a whole group could be doing as a unit and at one time. This would produce significant "waits" for individuals and thus slow down the movement.

Example: The teacher had just sent the Brownies from the reading circle and was about to get the Rockets (the target group) from seatwork to the reading circle. She stood up and said, "All right now, the Rockets put your seatwork away and get ready to come to the reading circle." (The Rockets were sitting at tables one and two.) "All right now, the children at table one stand up." The teacher waited as the children at table one stood up and remained standing at their table. "Johnny, you come up." Johnny walked to the reading circle and sat down there. "Billy, now you come up . . . Mary, now you come up . . . Suzanne, you come up . . . All right, now the children at table two stand up . . . Lemuel, now you come up . . . Robert, you come up . . . ," and so on, until all ten children comprising the Rockets were seated at the reading circle. This transition was categorized as group fragmentation because the target of the direction was a group and the teacher broke this target into ten separate targets, producing a "wait" for the other members and slowing down the movement from seatwork to reading. (It should be noted that taking turns while reading or reciting was not categorized as group fragmentation, for in recitation the separate individuals are the targets and are the performing units at the time.) In the transition summarized above, the group of Rockets is the target of the teacher's induction.

2. *Prop or actone fragmentation* was coded when the teacher fragmented a meaningful unit of behavior into smaller components and focused upon these separate sub-parts when the behavior could have been performed as a single, uninterrupted sequence. The sub-parts could be props or actones.

Example: The teacher was making a transition from spelling to arithmetic as follows: "All right everybody, I want you to close your spelling books. Put away your red pencils. Now close your spelling books. Put your spelling books in your desks. Keep them out of the way." Wait. "All right now. Take out your arithmetic books and put them on your desks in front of you. That's right, let's keep everything off your desks except your arithmetic books. And let's sit up straight. We don't want any lazy-bones do we? That's fine. Now get your black pencils and open your books to page sixteen."

All slowdowns were tallied by six-second intervals; a slowdown lasting six seconds would be scored as one unit; one of 7"-12" would be two units, and so on. A teacher's slowdown score consisted of the total number of the slowdown units in her recitation settings divided by the total number of units coded. This score was subtracted from one so that the teacher with the highest score would be the hypothesized "best" teacher in this respect; the one with the second highest score the second best, etc.

RESULTS RELATING SMOOTHNESS AND MOMENTUM TO CHILDREN'S BEHAVIOR

As can be seen in Appendix 4.1 both smoothness and momentum correlate significantly with children's behavior.

In recitation settings momentum (the absence of slowdowns) correlates with both work involvement (.656) and freedom from deviancy (.641). In seatwork settings, momentum correlates with freedom from deviancy (.490) but not with work involvement (.198). In general, momentum may be said to be more highly associated with children's behavior in recitation settings than in seatwork settings. Avoiding behaviors that impede movement in recitation settings tends to be the highest single determinant of successful behavior management in recitation settings.

Smoothness, by itself, is significantly associated with children's behavior in both recitation and seatwork settings. In recitation settings, smoothness correlates with both work involvement (.601) and freedom from deviancy (.489). In seatwork settings, smoothness correlates .382 with work involvement and .421 with freedom from deviancy. As is the case for momentum, the correlations tend to be higher for recitation than for seatwork settings.

Momentum and smoothness also correlate significantly with each other (.745). Teachers who engage in behaviors that produce jerky movement also engage in behaviors that slow down movement. Movement management may then be regarded as a meaningful and important dimension of classroom management.

Since momentum and smoothness are so highly correlated with each other, what happens when the effect of either one is statistically removed from the effects of the other? If we were to hold smoothness constant (hypothetically give all teachers the same score for smoothness) what would happen to the correlations between momentum and children's behavior? In recitation settings, the partialling out of smoothness from momentum does lower the correlations between momentum and children's behavior. However, the association of momentum still remains significant: .391 with work involvement and .476 with freedom from deviancy. However, if we remove the effects of momentum from smoothness the correlations between smoothness and children's behavior in recitation settings become statistically nonsignificant. When scores for momentum are held constant, smoothness correlates but .022 with freedom from deviancy and .222 with work involvement in recitation settings. By itself, then, momentum is more highly associated with children's behavior in recitation settings than is smoothness, by itself.

In seatwork settings, however, neither smoothness nor momentum are significantly correlated with children's behavior when the effects of the other is partialled out. In other words, and even though there are significant correlations between both momentum and smoothness and children's behavior in seatwork, these correlations are not "pure"—are not attributable to these separate measurements operating alone. Rather, the correlations between smoothness and children's behavior in seatwork are significant because momentum is also present. And, the correlation between momentum and children's deviancy in seatwork is significant because smoothness is also present.

Considering the reality—that teachers who avoid jerkiness also avoid impeding and slowing down movement—one must conclude that the dimension of movement management, including both smoothness and momentum is a significant dimension of classroom management. Within this dimension it is more important to maintain momentum by avoiding actions that slow down forward movement than it is to maintain smoothness by avoiding sudden starts and stops. And techniques of movement management are more significant in controlling deviancy than are techniques of deviancy management as such. In addition, techniques of movement management possess the additional value of promoting work involvement, especially in recitation settings.

6

MAINTAINING GROUP FOCUS: GROUP ALERTING, ACCOUNTABILITY, AND FORMAT

THE ISSUE OF GROUP FOCUS

A classroom teacher is not a tutor working with one child at a time. Even though she may work with a single child at times, her main job is to work with a group of children in one room at one time. Sometimes the group is the entire class and sometimes it is a subgroup or subgroups (as when she is at the reading circle with one group while another subgroup or other subgroups are at seatwork). Given this partial job analysis, it may be fruitful to see what techniques teachers use to maintain a group focus.

The following is a brief description of one reading subgroup:

Ten children are seated in a semi-circle in a reading group and Miss Smith is seated in front of them holding flash cards. Each card has a single word printed on it. The teacher announces, "Today we'll read a word and then think of a word that rhymes with it. We'll go around in a circle starting with Richard." Miss Smith turns toward Richard, who is seated at the left end of the semi-circle. She leans toward Richard, holding a flash card, and asks him, "What is this word, Richard?" Richard replies, "Nest." The teacher says, "That's right. And give me a word that rhymes with nest." Richard says, "Rest." Teacher responds, "That's fine." The teacher holds out another card and leans toward Mary, who is sitting at the left of Richard. "All right, Mary, what is this word?" Mary says,

109

"Rake." Teacher says, "That's right. Now give me a word that rhymes with rake." Mary replies, "Make." Teacher says, "That's fine." The teacher then removes another card, leans toward Ruth, who is sitting to the left of Mary, and asks, "Ruth, can you tell me what this word is?" Ruth replies, "Moon". This procedure continues until each child has had a turn pronouncing a word and giving a rhyming word.

Let us look at another teacher conducting the same kind of lesson. Miss Jones is seated in front of a subgroup of children at the reading circle. She is holding a stack of flash cards, saying, "Who can read the next one?" She pauses, holds up a card, looks around the group suspensefully and says, "John." John says, "Cook." The teacher says, "Fine. Now who can name a word that sounds like it?" The teacher pauses again, looks around, and calls on Mary. Mary says, "Cake." The teacher then asks, "Now who can think of a word that rhymes with cake?" She looks around and calls on Richard who replies with "make."

The above two lessons have essentially the same content—both require children to read a word and to name another word that rhymes with it. The manner of selecting reciters is conducted differently. Miss Smith has a predetermined order of reciters. Miss Jones selects reciters in a less predictable fashion: She raises a question, pauses, looks around, and then selects a reciter. In Miss Smith's class the children know who is and who is not going to be called on next, while in Miss Jones's class they do not. Does this result in the children in Miss Jones's class being more alert and being more "on their toes"?

There are also less divergent techniques of selecting reciters than the previous examples that vary from a completely predetermined sequence of reciters to a completely random sequencing of reciters. Mrs. Holly tends to select reciters by saying, "Suzanne, how much is eight plus four?" while looking at Suzanne. Mrs. Hudson tends to ask, "How much is eight plus four?", look around, then select a child to recite. Mrs. Holly tends to select the reciter before raising the question; Mrs. Hudson is inclined to raise the question before selecting the reciter.

Do these different techniques of selecting reciters create different degrees of alertness on the part of the children? And does it make any difference in the behavior of children? This managerial dimension was called *group alerting* to refer to the degree to which teachers keep children on their toes while selecting reciters.

Let us look at another aspect of group focus. Mrs. Friendly is in front of a subgroup of twelve children conducting a reading lesson. She is using a large piece of paper that has about forty words on it. She says, "I promised Albert yesterday that he could read the words today. Maybe tomorrow we'll have two more people read. Let's start with this, Albert." The teacher points to a word with a pointer and turns to Albert who reads aloud, "When." The teacher points to the next word and Albert reads, "Wagon." The teacher then says, "And what's this one, Albert?" as she points to the next word. Albert says, "Water." This continues until Albert finishes reading all forty words.

The above procedure of conducting a reading lesson may be contrasted with the reading lesson conducted by Mrs. Kind. Twelve children are in a semi-circle facing the blackboard where Mrs. Kind has printed some words. She says, "This is a word we had yesterday. What does it say?" She looks around momentarily and calls on Richard. Richard says, "Day." The teacher then points to another word and calls on Mary. Mary says, "Way." The teacher then says, "Now *everybody* read the next ones." The children recite in unison, as the teacher leans forward and looks around as they do. During this time she says, "I can't hear you, David. Louder." David reads more loudly. The teacher says, "That's fine. Now (as she points at a different word) what does this say, Muriel?" Muriel reads, "Work." The teacher then says, "*Everybody* read the next word," as she leans forward and cups her ear while looking around.

One will note that Mrs. Friendly selected but one reciter for the entire phonics lesson, and showed signs of attending only to him. She is providing Albert with considerable individual attention, but is not focusing on the group. Mrs. Kind, however, not only selected more than one reciter, but also attended to more than one reciter during the unison call-outs: She leaned forward, cupped her ear, looked around, and even picked out David, whom she couldn't hear, and asked him to read louder. This dimension of group focus was called *accountability.*

A child who recites is demonstrating what he knows or how well he can do something. The reciter is thus held accountable—the teacher gets to know what he is doing and he knows the teacher knows what he is doing regarding the particular task at the time. How many children in the group or subgroup know this? How many, in other words, are being held accountable? And does this influence the amount of work-involvement and deviancy?

Another aspect of group focus pertains to what the children who are not reciting are supposed to be doing when a child recites. This dimension may be exemplified by comparing two different addition lessons.

During Miss Fulton's arithmetic lesson each child has each of the ten digits on his desk along with a cardboard with slots. The teacher calls out an addition problem, such as "eight and four." Each child then attempts to place to answer in the slots with a "one" in one slot and a "two" next to it to his right, to make the sum of "12." The teacher then says, "All show!" Each child then raises his cardboard in the air to expose his answer to the teacher. This continues for all the addition problems in the lesson.

Mrs. Carter's addition lesson is conducted with a different format. Mrs. Carter calls on Richard to go to the board. Richard goes to the board and teacher says, "All right, Richard, show us how to add eight plus four." Richard writes eight and four with the sum of twelve. Teacher says, "That's fine. Now, Mabel, will you go to the board." Mabel goes to the board and does the next problem assigned by the teacher.

These two addition lessons manifest differences in what was called *format*. In Miss Fulton's lesson, all children, reciters and non-reciters, were actively engaged in doing something during each arithmetic problem: They were all selecting digits and placing them in the slots. In Mrs. Carter's class the only child who had something active to do was the one who was reciting at the board. The children at their desks had but to sit and listen while the one reciter wrote the problem on the board.

This dimension of group focus was called *format* to designate what other children were required to do when there was a reciter. There are, of course, varying degrees of participation required of nonreciters during a recitation. During a reading lesson involving the reading of a story, the children have a book with which to read along silently while one child is taking a turn reading aloud. Or, nonreciting children may have arithmetic problems to check in their work books while a child is answering the problem aloud. Do different formats of conducting recitations, entailing different degrees of concurrent participation on the part of nonreciters, make any difference in children's behavior?"

The following codes concerned with the maintenance of group focus were developed partly from hunches arrived at as a result of observing classrooms and the videotapes, and partly by comparing the managerial job of the teacher in a classroom with that of a tutor working with an individual child. The tutor has a relatively simple managerial job compared to the classroom teacher. Some reasons for this are: (1) The child working with a tutor is more likely to be actively involved performing an activity, whereas in a classroom situation, except for the child reciting, children are more likely to be placed in a passive, nonparticipating role. The child being tutored is either actively reciting and performing or else is an active listener in the sense of being the direct and only target of the tutor's actions. (2) The child in a tutorial situation is more likely to be on his toes and be alert since he knows he is the one to be called on. In a classroom, any one child is likely to be less alert since his chances of being called on are not as great. (3) The child in a tutorial situation is more likely to be checked and held accountable for his performances. The tutor knows what the child is doing at all times, and the child knows that the tutor knows.

The following codes were developed in order to deal with the issue of group focus by attempting to measure the degree to which teachers make the classroom situation similar to a tutorial situation in the above respects. The codes were limited to recitation sessions. There were three parts to this code: (1) Format—designed to get at the set-up of the activity in regard to the amount of participation required of members of the group; (2) Group Alerting—designed to ascertain the degree to which teachers keep children on their toes; and (3) Accountability—designed to measure how much the teacher holds the members of the group accountable for their performances.

Scoring group focus necessitates a somewhat different procedure than scoring for withitness, overlapping, and movement management. Unlike withitness or overlapping, the group focus does not relate to a specific type of event. Withitness relates to desist events only, and overlapping relates to desist events and child intrusion events. Group focus, however, relates to many kinds of events throughout all recitation sessions: the sequencing of reciters, the manner in which reciters are called on, the number of reciters called on, the degree to which the teacher goes out to listen, what nonreciters are supposed to be doing while another child is reciting, and a variety of other teacher techniques and manners.

Another difference in scoring for group focus is that, unlike some of the other dimensions, group focus has no clear either-or or right-wrong characteristics. In withitness, the teacher desists the correct deviant or doesn't; she comes in too late or on time. In both overlapping and desist events, the teacher either overlaps or does not. Group focus does not present a coder with such clear all or none, black or white choices. Is it a mistake to call on children to recite in a predetermined order, or is it "fair" in that all children get to recite the same number of times? Is it "bad" for Mrs. Friendly to concentrate on Albert during the phonics lesson because it limits accountability to Albert, or is it desirable in that it provides Albert with individual attention? Is it good to maintain suspense about who is to be called on because it may keep children on the alert, or is it undesirable because it may create too much tension?

Unlike the other dimensions, group focus occurs along a continuum over the total length of recitation periods. The format may even change within any single recitation session. In an arithmetic lesson, the teacher may change from checking problems in work books to explaining a new set of problems; in a reading circle she may change from having children take turns while reading a story to analyzing the phonics involved in some new words and the degree of group focus may vary dependent upon her style of conducting these subparts of a recitation. This is somewhat more complicated than, for example, the movement code, where specific teacher behaviors are tallied and timed: the teacher thrusts, dangles, fragments the group, nags, and so on.

The problem in scoring the group focus factors was to attend to the total stream and continuum of recitation sessions as well as to base the score upon specific, concrete teacher behaviors. Scoring, therefore, was accomplished for particular periods of time rather than for particular types of events. All the group focus factors were scored by 30-second intervals. The score for each time interval, however, was based upon particular, concrete behaviors. The score for any 30-second interval was, thereby, not markedly influenced (as in rating scales) by previous intervals or by a frame of reference obtained from other classrooms. The existence of videotapes, which enabled coders to replay the same intervals as many times as desirable, made this procedure possible.

The following codes for group focus are presented in order to provide the reader with the meaning of the three facets of group focus and with an idea of how we attempted to maintain a global continuum along with the specification of concrete behaviors, even though they may present the reader with more than he might care to know about the codes.

THE MEANING AND MEASUREMENT OF FORMAT

In recitation settings there is a certain formal set-up in respect of props and activity demands. The format code was designed to categorize the degree of participation required of those children not engaged in reciting (reading aloud, answering a question, demonstrating) at any particular time. What are nonperforming children required to do by way of participation when another child is reciting or performing? The format categories were:

High Participation

High participation by nonperformers was categorized when:

1. There was persistent concurrent active participation by all members of the group. To fit this category, all children are required to do a real individual performance simultaneously which involves an active, overt manipulation of some prop. An example of this is Miss Fulton's arithmetic lesson. (Mass unison responses—when a teacher asks all children to give an answer to a question in unison—were *not* coded here.)

2. There was mixed concurrent-active and concurrent-passive participation. In concurrent-passive participation one child is performing or reciting while all others are required to engage in some kind of concurrent performance or cognitive search beyond simple recognition. Examples: Several children work problems on the board while all other children work the same problems in their workbooks or on mimeographed sheets; or, while one child is reading a story aloud, the rest of the children are to read along

silently and are required to search for some issue in the story which they will be questioned about.

Moderate Participation

Moderate participation was categorized when there was concurrent-passive participation required of the nonreciters in the group. Example: Children in a reading group are to read along silently in a story but with directions to locate some word, picture, numeral, or event (simple recognition).

Teacher Lecture Recitation

This was a category used to designate formats where the teacher lectured or demonstrated while the children engaged in sporadic concurrent-active participation. Here, the teacher intersperses lectures or explanations with periods of active, inclusive recitation.

Low Participation

This format was categorized when concurrent participation was seldom required: One child recites while the others merely watch and listen. An example is Miss Carter's arithmetic lesson.

Anti-Format

Anti-format was coded when the teacher's conduct of the recitation precluded the children's achieving effective performance of the official task. This format obtained when the teacher gave ambiguous or conflicting directions (i.e., telling children to answer problems in their workbooks while she went to the board and talked about different problems) or when the teacher's actions interfered with children's assigned tasks (i.e., teacher engaged in a stream of irrelevant talk while children were supposed to take turns checking workbook problems).

Nothing-To-Do Format

This was coded when the predominant activity during a recitation was a *wait* with nothing to do. This empty waiting could be caused by a teacher's withdrawal (becoming "immersed" in talking with an intruding child while dropping the recitation group completely and without any directions or job to perform during her absence), or by the official format (each child has his own individual task that is separate from the others, and each gives his independent recitation and, after finishing, has nothing to do but wait until all the children have taken turns and completed their separate recitations).

THE MEANING AND MEASUREMENT OF GROUP ALERTING

Group alerting refers to the degree to which a teacher attempts to involve nonreciting children in the recitation task, maintain their attention, and keep them "on their toes" or alerted. Anything the teacher does that indicates an overt effort on her part to get more than the reciter attentive and involved was considered a group alerting cue. The group alerting score for a teacher was obtained by counting concrete positive alerting and negative (or anti) group alerting behaviors.

Positive Group Alerting Cues

Positive group alerting cues are those behaviors of a teacher that keep nonreciters on their toes while another child is reciting or before the selection of a new reciter. Positive group alerting cues were:

1. Any method used to create "suspense" before calling on a child to recite: pausing and looking around to "bring children in" before selecting a reciter; saying, "Let's see now, who can. . ." before calling on a reciter.
2. Keeping children in suspense in regard to who will be called on next; picking reciters "randomly" so that no child knows whether he will be called on next or not.
3. Teacher calls on different children frequently or maintains group focus: intersperses "mass unison" responses; says, "Let's put our thinking caps on; this might fool you;" asks group for show of hands before selecting a reciter.
4. Teacher alerts nonperformers that they might be called on in connection with what a reciter is doing: They may be called on if reciter makes a mistake; presignals children that they will be asked about recitation content in the immediate future.

5. Teacher presents new, novel, or alluring material into a recitation (a high attention value prop or issue).

Negative or Anti-group Alerting Cues

Negative group alerting cues were those behaviors of a teacher during a child's recitation, or preceding the selection of a new reciter, that reduced the involvement of nonreciters in a recitation session. These produced a lower degree of alertness on the part of nonreciters than that obtaining in ordinary, routine recitation sessions.

Negative group alerting cues were:

1. The teacher changes the focus of her attention away from the group and becomes completely immersed in the performance of the reciter; or directs a new question and subsequent attention to a single new reciter only, without any overt sign of awareness that there is a group.
2. The teacher prepicks a reciter or performer before the question is even stated.
3. The teacher has reciters perform in a predetermined sequence of turns. That is, children know beforehand that they are to read from left to right with the child at the far left reading first, then the child next to him, then the child next to him or her, and so on. (In contrast to a random selection of reciters, a child in this sequence knows ahead of time when he is not and when he is going to be called upon to recite.)

Scoring Group Alerting

Five categories of the degree of group alerting were judged and scored on a global basis for each 30-second recitation interval coded. These were:

1. *High*: An interval was scored as high if it contained three or more positive cues and no negative cues.
2. *Moderate*: An interval was scored as moderate if it contained two different positive cues and no negative cues.
3. *Low*: This was used to designate an interval containing a single positive cue.

4. *None*: An interval containing neither positive nor negative cues or where group alerting was judged to be mechanical or clearly artificial.

5. *Anti*: This was used when an interval contained one or more negative cues.[1]

THE MEANING AND MEASUREMENT OF ACCOUNTABILITY

Accountability refers to the degree to which the teacher holds the children accountable and responsible for their task performances during recitation sessions. This entails her doing something to get to know what the children are actually doing and to communicate to the children in some observable manner that she knows what they are doing. The degree to which she goes out to obtain this knowledge and to communicate it, is the degree to which she holds the children in the group accountable for their performances. A teacher's accountability is the number of children she makes accountable. Her accountability for a group may be from none of the children to all of the children in the group. (A "none" is actually possible, for a teacher may so behave as to manifest no awareness of even how a reciter is performing—she might be totally involved in feeding the fish when a child in a reading group is reciting.)

The most usual means of securing information is for the teacher to require children to produce or demonstrate work that is being done in the current setting and to check these demonstrations. The number of children whose performances are checked can serve as a basis for scoring her accountability.

Accountability Cues

Following are the kinds of behaviors to be noted in arriving at judgments of a teacher's accountability:

1. Teacher asks children to hold up their props exposing performances or answers in such a manner as to be readily visible to the teacher.

[1]Whenever an interval contained both positive and negative cues, the predominant cue was used for that interval and the less predominant one was, by convention, "added" to the next interval in order that it be given credit.

2. Teacher requires children to recite in unison while the teacher shows signs of actively attending to the recitation.
3. Teacher brings other children into the performance of a child reciting. (Teacher says, "Jimmy, you watch Johnny do that problem and then tell me what he did right or wrong.")
4. Teacher asks for the raised hands of children who are prepared to demonstrate a performance and requires some of them to demonstrate.
5. Teacher circulates and checks products of nonreciters during a child performance.
6. Teacher requires a child to demonstrate and checks his performance.

Scoring Accountability Cues

Using the above cues, or any other obvious ones, that a teacher was engaging in checking behavior, coders made a global judgment of the teacher's accountability according to the proportion of children in a group who were checked during a given 30-second interval. The accountability was judged as follows:

1. *High*: A high rating was given to a teacher when she checked the entire group as individuals; e.g., teacher asked all children to hold up their props, showing their answers clearly, and demonstrated her awareness of correct and incorrect performances by comments or other signals.

A high rating was also given when the teacher checked the performing subgroup as well as some nonperformers, or otherwise checked at least half of the group as individuals; e.g., a row of children performed arithmetic problems at the blackboard and were checked individually by the teacher as she also looked at the work of the nonperforming children who were at their seats.

2. *Moderate*: A moderate rating was given when a teacher checked 25 percent to 50 percent of the group as individuals, or the entire group as a whole; e.g., teacher circulated among performers and nonperformers, checking the visible products of at least 25 percent of the group. Or, teacher asked for mass unison answers or corrections and checked on these responses. Or, teacher checked at least 25 percent of the group as individuals, each child giving an individual response.

3. *Low*: A low rating was given when a teacher checked less than 25 percent of the group as individuals, or called for mass unison without apparent check on individual performances; e.g., teacher circulated and checked several children on first example, then several others on second example, etc. Or, teacher circulated and looked at papers of nonperformers while listening to a child recite. Or, teacher checked only on the child demonstrating the task. Or, teacher asked for mass unison but gave no cue of checking the performances of the children in the group.

4. *None*: A rating of none was given when the teacher gave no cue of actually checking the work of any child; e.g., as a child recited the teacher simply walked around without any evidence of her attending to the performance of the reciter or of checking other children. Or, the teacher did not actively attend to the performance of the child reciting. Or, the teacher called for a mass unison response but did not attend to their responses. Or, teacher asked for show of hands or for children to say "yes" or "no" in answer to a question regarding their performing correctly but did not ask for a checkable demonstration.

An Additional Measure of Accountability

In addition to rating accountability by means of the above behavioral cues the coders tallied the number of different reciters. Any time a new and different reciter was called upon to recite during a recitation session this was tallied. Thus, one could count the number of different children who were individually checked during a recitation session. A score based upon the number of different reciters per minute was also used as a measure of the teacher's accountability.

SCORING THE GROUP FOCUS DIMENSIONS

Except for counting the number of different reciters whenever this occurred, coders rated the various group focus dimensions by 30-second intervals. Each 30 seconds of a recitation session was scored as a unit for the duration of a recitation session.

The score for format was computed by summing the high, moderate, and lecture-recitation intervals and dividing this sum by the total number of intervals coded. Thus, the greater the number of these intervals relative to the low, anti-format, and nothing to do format intervals, the higher a teacher's format score.

One score for accountability was computed by summing the intervals containing high and moderate accountability cues and dividing this sum by the total number of intervals. Another score for accountability was based upon the number of different reciters per minute of time.

The score for group alerting was computed by assigning a weight to each interval coded. A high group alerting interval was scored five, moderate was scored four, low was scored three, none was scored two, and anti was scored one. These scores were summed and divided by the number of intervals coded to obtain a teacher's score for group alerting.

THE RESULTS RELATING GROUP FOCUS DIMENSIONS TO CHILDREN'S BEHAVIOR

Format scores did *not* correlate significantly with either work involvement or deviancy in either recitation or seatwork settings. It should be emphasized that the format scores were based upon the official, formal set-up of the various recitation sessions and were *not* based upon how the teacher went about actually conducting the session. Thus, the session did or did not have props (books, cards, workbooks, mimeograph sheets) which nonperforming children were to be engaged with while a reciter performed; or the format called for a combination of recitation and lecture or did not; and so on. Format scores are thus based upon the officially designated set-up regarding props and the role of nonperformers. The scores are not based upon how the teacher actually managed what was formally required.

One may conclude that the officially designated formats of recitation sessions, in and of themselves, do not appreciably lead to work involvement or restrain deviancy. As far as the behavior of children is concerned, the manner in which a teacher goes about carrying through an official format is more significant than the format itself.

Group alerting is significantly related to children's behavior. In recitation settings, the correlation is.603 with work involvement and

.442 with freedom from deviancy. In seatwork, group alerting is weakly correlated (.290; $p = .05$) and with freedom from deviancy only.

It may be said, then, that teachers who maintain a group focus by engaging in behaviors that keep children alerted and on their toes are more successful in inducing work involvement and preventing deviancy than are teachers who do not. This aspect of teacher style is more significant in recitation settings than in seatwork settings.

Accountability is also associated with children's behavior. There were two different scores for accountability: One consisted of global judgments based upon specific behavioral cues (circulating among nonreciters, requesting demonstrations of performances from nonreciters, etc.), and the other consisted of a count of different reciters. Both measures correlated in the same direction and approximate size with work involvement and deviancy. Accordingly, only the simpler measure was used. The correlations presented in this book are the ones using the number of different reciters per minute as the measure of accountability.

The correlations between accountability and children's behavior were significant in recitation settings only. These were: .494 with work involvement and .385 with freedom from deviancy. In recitation settings, then, it does make a difference whether teachers demonstrate to the group that they know what the children are doing about the ongoing tasks. A teacher may do this by calling upon different reciters with sufficient frequency, or by engaging in other behaviors, such as attending to nonperformers during a recitation, that demonstrate to the group that she knows what they are doing.[2]

The correlation between accountability and group alerting is also significant: .494. Teachers who engage in those behaviors comprising the group alerting score also tend to manifest accountability. Both indicate behaviors that evidence the maintenance of a group focus and of not becoming immersed in single persons to the point of neglecting the recitation group.

[2]Accountability may be seen as equivalent to withitness, except that withitness refers to communicated knowledgeability about behavior and misbehavior, while accountability refers to communicated knowledgeability about children's task performances during specific recitation sessions.

Of the two, group alerting appears to be the more significant aspect of group focus. The correlations between group alerting and children's behavior are not only higher but they remain significant when the effects of accountability are removed by partial correlations. When the effects of accountability are eliminated, the correlations between group alerting and children's behavior remain significant: .475 with work involvement (reduced from .603), and .313 with freedom from deviancy (reduced from .442). When the contribution of group alerting is removed, the correlation between accountability and work involvement is .283 (reduced from .494), and the correlation with freedom from deviancy is a statistically insignificant .213 (reduced from .385). And, while both of these aspects of group focus increase work involvement and reduce deviancy, it would seem to be more significant to keep children alerted and on their toes than to check on them. Teachers who are successful in managing overt behavior, however, tend to do both.

7

PROGRAMMING
TO AVOID SATIATION

The next question has to do with the nature of the activities programmed in the classrooms. What are the groups of children required to do—what is the teacher moving them into and out of? Does the nature of the classroom activity program relate to work involvement and deviancy?

Answers to the above question entail an analysis of the curriculum which is clearly beyond the scope and data of this study. Moreover, within the school systems studied, the overall curriculum was much the same and the same major books and materials were used for the different classrooms of the same grade. However, even within the same grades of the same school, teachers do vary in what they emphasize, in how they sequence the activities, and in what they do beyond the school's basic curricular commonalities.

The Videotape Studies distinguished two gross kinds of academic activities: recitation and seatwork. The children's behaviors did differ in these settings. There was more work involvement and less deviancy in recitation settings, where the teacher was actively conducting the sessions, than in seatwork settings, where the children were working pretty much on their own.

The magnitude of the correlations between teachers' behavior and children's behavior differed as between recitation and seatwork settings. For example, teacher momentum correlated more with

125

work involvement in recitation settings than with work involvement in seatwork settings. On the other hand, programmed variety correlated more with work involvement in seatwork settings than it correlated with work involvement in recitation settings. The best combination of teacher style ingredients conducive to successful management in recitation settings is different from the best combination of teacher style ingredients conducive to successful management in seatwork settings.

Beyond this gross distinction between recitation and seatwork activities, what can we measure about the classroom programs that make a difference in how children behave? The videotapes do not enable one to measure certain commonly cited attributes of an activity program such as interest value, meaningfulness to everyday lives, difficulty placement, appropriateness to developmental levels, and the like. However, we did attempt some categorizations of the activity programs that were codable and around which there were differences between the classrooms.

The dimensions of activity programming that we coded related to the issue of psychological satiation. Satiation is defined by Kurt Lewin[12] as the change of valence of an activity due to repetition. Researches show that pure repetition not only changes the valence of an activity but also reduces the quality of work. Repetition produces changes from positive valence (being liked) to negative valence (being disliked). With increasing repetition, the activity becomes less and less positive then more and more negative. This satiation is a process rather than an all-or-none state of affairs. There are degrees of satiation dependent upon the amount of repetition and the corresponding amount of decrease in positive valence or the amount of increase in negative valence. One may, for example, still like an activity yet be partly satiated (one just likes the activity less than one did prior to the repetition).

The process of satiation also produces predictable changes in overt behavior such as: the spontaneous introduction of variations in the activity; decreasing quality of work; increasing number of mistakes; and a dedifferentiation or break-down in the meaning of the activity. An example of dedifferentiation: A student is required to write the sentence, "I will not talk," fifty times. One sign of satiation is the student's beginning to make a column of "I's," then a column of "will's," and so on. The meaning of the sentence is thus dedifferentiated: It is no longer writing a complete sentence but is, rather, a listing of separate words.

Overt manifestations of decreased liking or increased dislike for the activity are manifest in tendencies of the person to show less involvement in the activity and more inclinations to get out of it or to "leave the field." Some behavioral signs are: more frequent and longer pauses, more looking elsewhere, more escapes (tying shoe laces, sharpening pencils, combing hair, overt restlessness, etc.). These behavioral signs of the process of satiation should be manifest in lower work involvement or higher deviancy scores.

**THE MEASUREMENT OF THE SATIATION POTENTIAL
OF CLASSROOM PROGRAMS**

It should be emphasized that the Videotape Studies did not provide us with data that measures satiation directly. There were no direct measures of the satiation values of the activities nor of the children's satiation symptoms. We could only attempt to get at some indirect cues to ascertain whether the management of repetitiousness has any bearing upon work involvement and deviancy scores.

A feeling of progress is the most essential variable influencing the rate of satiation. Satiation does not occur, or occurs very slowly, when there is a feeling of progress since the essential condition for producing satiation is repetitiousness: doing the same thing over and over without getting anywhere. When there is a feeling of progress there is no feeling of repetition and no consequent satiation. The videotapes did not enable one to ascertain whether or not, or how much, the children were experiencing a feeling of progress or a feeling of repetitiousness.

Nor did we have direct measures of behavioral signs of satiation. We did not zoom in on individual children to secure data about the time at which they began to introduce variations in their performances; the size and frequency of these variations; the rate and size of mistakes; the rate and duration of pauses; and other direct signs of the degree of satiation present.

The following attempts to relate satiation management to the behavior of children, then, entail only indirect and gross measures of the satiation potentials of classroom programs, as well as gross and indirect measures of the behavioral signs of satiation.

The Duration of Activities

One question about the programmed activities in the school day has to do with the length of activities. A common concept, implicitly related to satiation, is that of "attention span"—the length of time that a child can remain actively involved in an activity before becomming "bored," restless, and desirous of quitting.

The videotapes did provide data for determining the length of time teachers had children engage in academic activities. Three measures were obtained: the average time spent in all the academic sessions, the average time spent in recitation sessions, and the average time spent in seatwork sessions.

Teachers were then ranked on the basis of the average length of time that they required the children to remain in academic sessions. The three rankings were correlated with work involvement and deviancy in both seatwork and recitation settings.

None of the correlations between the duration of academic activities and children's behavior were significant. The overall average duration of activities did not correlate with either deviancy or work involvement in either seatwork or recitation settings (4 correlations). The average duration of recitation sessions did not correlate with either work involvement or deviancy in recitation settings (2 correlations). Nor did the average duration of seatwork sessions correlate with either work involvement or deviancy in seatwork settings (2 correlations). All the correlations were in the order of zero.

Programming for "attention span," when this is simply seen as the length of academic sessions, is not a significant dimension of classroom management. The time spent in an activity does not, in and of itself, constitute even an indirect measure of satiation management.

Positive and Negative Progress Cues

We attempted to secure another indirect measure of satiation management by noting whether teachers engaged in behaviors that might relate to repetitiousness or a feeling of progress. Does a teacher do anything beyond the usual routine in a recitation session that would be likely to produce either a clear feeling of repetitiousness or a clear feeling of progress in an academic activity?

The code for progress cues consisted of three categories:

1. *Routine* was coded when the teacher engaged in ordinary and usual kinds and amounts of behavior relating to progress or repetition: She did nothing special to induce feelings of progress nor did she impose special repetitiousness during recitations.

Cues for coding routine were: having children take turns in reading parts of a story in sequence; having reciters give answers to workbook problems in sequence; going through a list of words, sentences, problems; mechanical, routine acknowledgements of children's recitation by "next" and "yes;" positive evaluations of *current* performances by "That's fine" and "That's very good Jimmy." Such routine techniques of changing reciters, going over a sequence of items in a story or workbook, acknowledging the quality of an immediately preceding recitation, and the like, are usual and ordinary behaviors of teachers while conducting a recitation session—they neither induce special feelings of progress nor occasion unusual repetitiveness.

2. *Positive cues* were noted whenever a teacher did something beyond the immediate call of duty to get a child or group to feel that they were making progress and accomplishing something in the activity. (Ordinary acknowledgements, evaluations, or compliments regarding an immediately preceding performance were *not* coded as positive cues but were coded as routine.)

Positive cues were: explicitly building on a previous day's work: "Yesterday we learned . . . now we're going to see if we can . . .;" pointing out some real improvement between the current performance and previous work: "You got two more problems right today than you did yesterday;" bringing in clear enrichments, or interspersing genuinely challenging, yet accomplishable subtasks that contribute to the ongoing activity and reduce the feeling of repetitiousness.

3. *Negative cues* were coded whenever a teacher repeated an explanation or demonstration beyond what was necessary for clarity, or when she had a child or children repeat a performance when it was already correct. Example: the teacher had children read separate words from flash-cards. She had one child pronounce a

word, then another child pronounce the same word, then another, until each child in the reading circle read the same word.

Coders categorized the teacher's behavior as routine, positive, or negative in each 30-second interval of recitation settings. They were scored in four different ways: (1) The percentage of intervals containing positive cues; (2) The percentage of intervals containing negative cues; (3) A ratio of positive to negative plus neutral cues; and (4) A ratio of negative to positive plus neutral cues.

This attempt to secure some indirect measure of satiation management during recitation sessions was not successful. There simply was not enough variation of scores among the different teachers to justify correlating these with children's behaviors. The entries for all teachers were almost exclusively routine. There were very few instances of clear progress point-outs nor of repetitiveness. For example, of forty-nine teachers, twenty-seven had two or fewer 30-second intervals throughout all their recitation sessions in which negative cues appeared. In other words, most teachers spent less than one minute in what was judged as unnecessary repetitiousness during recitation sessions. There was an equal scarcity of events in which teachers did something beyond routine to create a special feeling of progress.

VALENCE AND CHALLENGE AROUSAL

A valence and challenge arousal code was designed to see what teachers do about satiation management in the way of attempting to enhance the attraction or challenge of the classroom activities. These are direct attempts by teachers to get the children more enthusiastic, involved, or curious about academic activities.

Valence and challenge arousal was coded at all transition points. What did the teacher do beyond designation and clarification to produce a motivational push towards the task to follow? An additional push could be made by: (1) showing genuine zest and enthusiam; (2) making a statement pointing out that the activity possesses special positive valence such as, "This next one is going to be fun; I know you'll enjoy it," or (3) making a statement pointing out that the activity possesses some special intellectual challenge. Example: "You're going to need your thinking caps for the next one, it's tricky."

Valence and challenge arousal was scored by computing the percent of a teacher's transitions that contained some such motivational enhancements. Transitions that were judged to be mechanical or "fake" or which were not in actuality either somewhat enjoyable or intellectually challenging were not counted as containing valence or challenge arousal.

These efforts at maintaining positive valence for academic activities were somewhat successful in increasing work involvement and reducing deviancy in both recitation and seatwork settings. The correlations between scores in valence and challenge arousal and children's behavior were somewhat low, ranging from .308 to .372, but were statistically significant.

Variety

We next attempted to approach the issue of satiation management by devising a measure of variety for a classroom's activity program. Since satiation means "doing the same thing over and over," variety should relate to the rate of satiation. The greater the variety of activities in a unit of time, the less rapidly should the process of satiation occur. Is the amount of programmed variety a significant determinant of managerial success in classrooms?

In order to answer this question, it is necessary to obtain a measure of variety. This entails determining how different one activity is from another. Doing arithmetic problems at seatwork is some change from doing spelling words at seatwork. However, there are also some similarities between these activities: children are sitting, writing, at the same location, etc. It is obvious that more change is involved in a transition from "spelling seatwork" to "outdoor recess" than there is change in a transition from "spelling seatwork" to "arithmetic seatwork." Most children would probably say that there is a greater difference between spelling and outdoor recess than there is between spelling and arithmetic. Or, most children would judge spelling to be more similar to arithmetic than to outdoor recess. In order to somewhat justify and quantify these judgments one would have to specify ways in which the activities are both similar and different and be able to say that there are X number of similarities and Y number of differences between them. Then, one could say that there are X number of differences between spelling and outdoor recess compared to *Y* number of differences between spelling seatwork and arithmetic seatwork. Such a procedure might not be complete in the sense of categorizing all ways in which activities might be described, but it would suffice to measure the relative amount of difference between various activities, providing that the categories related to meaningful aspects of activities.

This procedure was followed in developing a code for variety. Each classroom activity was described by means of each of eight characteristics. The amount of difference between any one activity and another could then be measured by counting the number of characteristics in which they differed. The categories used in describing each activity were: academic content; covert behavior mode; teacher's presentation pattern; kinds of props; group configuration; child responsibility; overt behavior mode; and location.[1] The descriptions of these categories follows.

Content designates the name of the activity. This is what a child would say was going on: that he was doing arithmetic, spelling, reading, geography, etc. The different categories used were:

Story reading, plots, narration. These have a distinct plot.
Phonics words, meanings, sounds. These entail mechanical, rote recognition.
Grammar, sentence structure, compositions.
Spelling.
Handwriting; copying.
Arithmetic.
Geography.
Current events.
Science.
Reviews and overviews.
Miscellaneous contents. Content uncertain, but have different props and are different from preceding content.

---

[1]Most of these categories were borrowed from those used by Barker and Wright in characterizing behavior settings. Others, such as academic content and teacher's presentation pattern, were added because of their uniqueness to classroom activity settings.

Art.

Music.

Poetry and stories.

Show and tell.

Informal discussions not related to any other category.

Games not related to any other category, and exercises.

Rest, waits, and routine.

Filler, if present. These are not work required of all children, but are options for those who complete regular assignment in seatwork.

Covert behavior mode refers to the type and level of intellectual function required by the task. What level of intellectual challenge does the task demand? The code is arranged from low to high intellectual challenge, and consists of the following categories:

1. Requires perseveration or attention only. Children are required to listen only, or to copy something (words, sentences, numbers).
2. Requires the rehearsal or use of a specific skill. This includes: simple oral reading; phonics drills; simple recognition or naming; adding numbers; coloring.
3. Requires comprehension, selective recognition, or memory. This includes: recalling part of a story; reading with a "search" for certain kinds of items; answering questions (orally or in writing) that require more than simple recognition.
4. Requires thought and abstract decisions. This includes puzzle problems, sentence problems in arithmetic, categorizing things that belong together or don't belong together in "think and do" exercises.
5. Requires creativity. This requires individual expression and the production of different products by different children, such as, "Draw your favorite part of a story."

Teacher's lesson presentation pattern is described on the basis of what the teacher is predominantly doing during the session. She could be:

Demonstrating or giving routine instructions.

Testing.

Reading a story or leading in the singing of a song.

Drilling, quizzing, and giving instructions as a lesson.

Engaging in casual discussion and participating with the children.

Circulating, supervising, checking papers; this occurs during supervised seatwork sessions.

Watching and observing.

Engaged with another group. This occurs for the nonsupervised seatwork subgroups where the teacher is working with a recitation subgroup (mostly reading groups at a reading circle).

Props used in the lesson are categorized primarily on the basis of ordinary and prevalent versus unique and rarely used. The categories used were:

1. Ordinary props (pencils, paper, book) or no props are being used.
2. Standard props that are generally available or are being used by only a portion of the group being scored, e.g., blackboard, maps, charts. Or, props being used are not used most of the time, such as weekly readers, song books, beads and marbles in academic games, coloring books.
3. Unique prop (one of a kind) that is standard equipment in this classroom, e.g., phonograph, single maps, or charts.
4. Unique prop (one of a kind) but available for less than a week in this classroom, e.g., show and tell objects, projector, magazine.

Group configuration refers to whether the child, at the time, was part of a total class group or a smaller subgroup. These categories are:

1. In subgroup W, X, Y, or Z.
2. In entire class.
3. In subgroup different from previous subgroup.

Child responsibility refers to the predominant role played by the child in setting the pace for the movement of the activity. These categories are:

1. Child passive and/or listening.
2. Reading aloud, answering teacher's questions or alerted to answer questions. Manipulates props while teacher asks questions, e.g., taking turns at blackboard when in a session of checking arithemetic problems.
3. Sets own pace as to time, place, and what he does within designated content.
4. Participating in unison activities, informal discussions, games.
5. Helps set pace for at least one other child, e.g., pairing to work with flash cards or group projects.

Overt behavior mode describes the predominant overt behavior of the group or subgroup having to do with sedentary to vigorously active. The categories coded are:

1. Reading, listening, oral reading by turns.
2. Writing, tracing, checking papers, small space drawing.
3. Large space drawing.
4. Manipulating props or small muscular movement of own body: work with cards, abacus, writing on blackboard, engaged in academic games.
5. Walking, running, engaged in large muscle movement.

Location refers to the geographical location of the children. Those designated were:

1. Own desk
2. Around teacher
3. Other location in classroom
4. Outside of room

The Scoring of Variety

Each activity was coded for each of the eight characteristics. If a subgroup of children made a transition from seatwork arithmetic to the reading circle, the seatwork arithmetic was coded for eight categories and the reading group was scored for the same eight categories. All activities in the school day were coded in the sequence in which they occurred. Changes between any two adjacent activities could vary from one through eight. The differences between all temporally adjacent activities were then summed.

The sum of these changes was determined for each classroom and this sum was divided by the total time consumed by these activities. This score represents a combination of variety and contrast: The variety score is increased (the dividend decreased) by increasing the variety of activities and by increasing the amount of difference between temporally adjacent activities. Rather then represent the average duration of activities, these scores represent the average duration of activities without change. A score of ten in seatwork, for example, could mean that a seatwork session lasted 10 minutes, or that it lasted 20 minutes but had two changes in it, or that it lasted 30 minutes but had three changes in it, and so on. The measure is thus not concerned with time as such, but with the amount of variety experienced per unit of time. If the teacher provided official activities for children when their official seatwork assignments were completed these "fillers" were also added to the variety scores. We reasoned that making available permissible activities for children to engage in after an official assignment is completed constitutes an antisatiation technique.

Some Preliminary Findings Relating to Variety

In the initial Videotape Study, thirty classrooms were videotaped for one-half day each and both upper and lower elementary school grades were included. All measures and correlations were analyzed separately for both emotionally disturbed children and non-emotionally disturbed children.

When correlating variety scores with children's behavior, 64 different correlations were obtained due to the fact that tables were developed for seatwork as well as for recitation; for grades 1–2 as well as for grades 3–5; for deviancy as well as for work involvement; and for emotionally disturbed children as well as for the others.

No significant positive correlations were found between the amount of variety in a classroom's half day and the behavior of children. Of 64 correlations, 26 were negative, and three of these were significant at the .05 level, a finding that could be accounted for by chance alone.

This absence of any positive correlations between programmed variety and work involvement or freedom from deviancy was puzzling to us and forced us to rethink the issue. It occurred to us that our variety score included both academic and nonacademic activities. One might reason that recess, "Simon Says," and other nonacademic parts of the school day were somewhat equivalent to "coffee breaks" in a work setting. These are not parts of the work but are temporary escapes from it. These breaks from work may make the total work situation more tolerable but do not actually change the valence of the work as such: Thus the dislike for "tightening bolts over and over" may not be decreased by an unrelated coffee break. Variety in the actual job content, however, might reduce the rate of satiation.

Accordingly, a variety score was developed that was based only on school-unique activities: those activities that most children would perceive as concerned with learning or skill development (reading, arithmetic, science, social studies, etc.). Nonacademic activities such as rest, physical exercise, nonacademic games, and recess were excluded from the variety scores.

The correlations between overall learning related variety (recitation plus seatwork) and children's behavior were higher than those obtained between children's behavior and overall variety for all activities. Of sixty-four pairs of correlations, fifty-nine were higher when learning variety only was used as a measure of variety. And, except for a few negative correlations for the upper grades only, all were positive. However, significant positive correlations were obtained only in seatwork settings, and only in all grades combined or for grades 1 and 2 only. Taken separately, none of the correlations for the upper grades were statistically significant.

We then proceeded to obtain a variety score for seatwork activities only and correlated these seatwork variety scores with children's behavior in seatwork. For Grades 1 and 2 the correlation between seatwork variety and work involvement was .827 ($N = 11$)

and for freedom from deviancy was .973. For grades 3–5 the correlations between seatwork variety and children's behavior in seatwork were negative : -.667 with work involvement and -.667 with freedom from deviancy ($N = 9$).

This preliminary exploration indicates that programming to reduce satiation by learning-related variety is a significant dimension of calssroom management. This aspect of programming a day's activity, however, may have to be planned differently for younger then for older children. It may well be that felt progress in learning is a more important antisatiation factor for the older children than for the younger children. Experienced variety may be relatively more salient for the younger children. The older children might require activities of sufficient length to enable them to experience progress and mastery. Activities that are terminated too quickly may not enable them to experience this mastery.

It should be noted that all the other dimensions of teacher style studied in the first Videotape Study showed no differences between the younger and older children. Smoothness, withitness, and overlapping correlated in the same direction and approximately the same magnitude with work involvement, deviancy, and deviancy-contagion, for both grades 1–2 and grades 3–5.

The results pertaining to variety are, at this point, tentative. Due to age differences as well as differences between seatwork and recitation settings, necessitating treating the settings and grades separately, the number of cases available for correlations was quite small. The second Videotape Study recorded first-and second-grade classrooms only, and recorded them for a full day each. We decided to record for a full day each in order to increase the likelihood of obtaining both seatwork and recitation settings for all classrooms.

The Results of the Second Videotape
Study Relating to Variety

Variety was scored in much the same manner as in the preliminary Videotape Study. There was one modification. A slightly greater weight was placed on the role of covert behavior mode. A value of minus one was placed on any activity that required no intellectual challenge, such as copying words or numbers. A point for variety was added if an activity had an intellectual challenge beyond simple skill rehearsal: required abstract decision or creativity. The theory behind this scoring is that activities that require perseveration only are more quickly satiated than activities that require thought and judgment.

The correlations between programmed learning-related variety and children's behavior are presented in Appendix 4.1. These are in essential agreement with the findings obtained from the preliminary study. Seatwork variety correlates with behavior in seatwork: .516 with work involvement and .276 with freedom from deviancy. In fact, seatwork variety correlates higher with work involvement in seatwork than any other single dimension of teacher style. Moreover, an analysis by means of partial correlations reveals that the correlation between seatwork variety and work involvement in seatwork is not reduced when the effects of any of the other dimensions of teacher style are eliminated.

Programmed variety does not correlate with behavior in recitation settings. Whatever effect variety might have upon behavior in recitation settings is overshadowed by the effects of the other dimensions of teacher style and by the predominance of routine progress management by all teachers in recitation sessions. Routine progress management, however, may be inadequate to produce appropriate behavior in children when movement is retarded by slowdowns or disrupted by jerkiness.

8

CONCLUDING COMMENTS

The preceding researches were attempts to secure answers to a practical problem of classroom teachers—that of classroom discipline. How should a teacher handle a child who misbehaves? Since a classroom teacher must deal with a group, the question was rephrased to include the group effects of disciplinary actions. This was called the *ripple effect*. In what ways does a teacher's technique of handling a misbehaving pupil influence *other* pupils in the classroom?

The author would like to summarize what he has learned as a result of his efforts and of those of the many persons working with him. These learnings relate to research methodology as well as to the management of behavior in classrooms.

The first question raised was whether or not there is a ripple effect. Are students who are not targets of a disciplinary event affected by it? And if they are affected, in what ways are they affected? The second question is whether different qualities of teachers' desists produce different kinds of effects. For example, does a desist with anger have different ripple effects than a desist without anger? Preliminary studies gave affirmative answers to both of the above questions. Systematic observations conducted during the first week of kindergarten, and experiments with college, high school, and elementary school students *all* showed a ripple effect

140

and *all* showed that variations in desist qualities produced different kinds of ripple effects. For example, in the Kindergarten Study, ripple effects were evidenced and were also influenced by the clarity, firmness, and anger of the teachers' desists. Desists with clarity produced more appropriate behavior and less deviancy on the part of audience children than desists without clarity. Desists with firmness produced the same ripple effects as did those with clarity but only for audience children who were themselves deviant or interested in deviancy at the time. Desists with anger and/or punitiveness produced work disruption and signs of emotional upset, but didn't change the conformity or deviancy of the audience children. We thus also learned that anger is not an intensification of firmness but that it is a different quality with different effects.

The results from the Kindergarten Study were not supported by a similar study conducted in a camp. There were no discernible ripple effects in camp—nor did variations in counselors' desist techniques make any difference in how audience campers reacted. (The only quality of a desist that made a difference was high attraction with novelty. If a counselor desisting Jim talked about a watermelon party, then John paid a little more attention to the desist event than he otherwise would. But John did not change his conformity or deviancy.)

The differences between the Kindergarten and Camp Studies were partly explained by the fact that these are different milieus. Interviews revealed that children have different concepts and concerns about misbehavior in camp, home, and school milieus. The kinds of misconducts they talk about for home, camp, and school are quite different. They also see different kinds of consequences for misconduct in camp, home, and school. Examples of some of the differences: Children are more preoccupied with breaking things at home than at school and are more concerned with rule violations at school than at home; there was more aggressivity in the camp misconducts than in the school misconducts. What is more, children perceive the roles of parents, teachers, and camp counselors in issues of misbehavior as quite different. Some of the differences are: Parents suffer (worry, have to pay repair bills) while teachers do not; parents are seen as punishing more severely and with more corporal punishment while teachers are seen as more inclined to explain realistic consequences.

Milieu differences are further apparent in the way children describe camp counselors and teachers. What they see as salient for one role is different from what they see as important for another. Camp counselors, for example, are perceived predominantly in terms of "gratuitous giver" (brings us candy) while teachers are rarely described in this dimension.

These findings taught us that studies of adult-child relationships, of which discipline is one facet, cannot be separated from the milieus in which they occur and the major roles of central adults in these milieus. An understanding of teacher-child relationships must be based upon research conducted with teachers in classroom settings. We are not justified in arriving at conclusions about teacher-child relationships in classrooms from studies conducted with parents in homes, counselors in offices, psychotherapists in clinics, or recreation leaders in recreation settings.

There were also differences between findings obtained from experiments in simulated classrooms and findings obtained from interviews and questionnaires conducted about real classrooms. In simulated classroom groups, or in actual classroom groups with an experimental teacher conducting the classroom for the first time, different desist techniques *did* produce different ripple effects. For example, task-focused desists ("You can't learn if you play with paper clips") produced more favorable ripple effects than approval-focused techniques ("I don't like children who play with paper clips").

In contrast, interviews conducted with high school students about their actual classrooms showed that qualities of desist techniques did *not* relate to ripple effects. Ripple effects *were* related to students' degree of motivation to learn the subject being taught and to their liking for the teacher. The prevailing variable of motivation was related to task-connected ripple effects such as inclination to behave better after a desist directed at another. The prevailing variable of liking for the teacher predicted to ripple effects related to evaluative judgments of the teacher, such as fairness. These prevailing variables or commitments did *not* correlate with ripple effects in experiments.

The contrast between the results obtained from the interviews and those obtained from the experiments provided another learning. We learned that the commitments of a subject in an experiment are different from the kinds of commitments that develop in real life situations. We also learned that simulated conditions may teach us something about the psychology of first impressions. These initial perceptions and reactions may be quite different from the perceptions and reactions to similar events in ongoing real situations.

These learnings about the qualities and determinants of ripple effects led us to utilize a more ecologically oriented approach to the study of classroom management. We decided to accumulate videotapes of naturally occurring classrooms. This was done more in a spirit of inquiry to see what we could learn than in a spirit of debate to see what hypothesis we could test. Videotapes would enable us to study what was occurring and not merely what was perceptually outstanding, interesting, or in line with some existing hypotheses. Moreover, they could be replayed over and over and thus enable the measurement of many different coexisting variables as well as variables not thought of at the time of data gathering.

An analysis of the desist events observed in the videotaped classrooms showed that the qualities of desists bore *no* relationship to children's reactions. The finding of no relationship between teachers' desist techniques and the behavior of children held for the immediate reaction of children to specific desists, as well as for the overall amount of deviancy and deviancy-contagion present in a classroom.

This latter learning involved unlearning on my part, in the sense of having to replace the original question by other questions. Questions about disciplinary techniques were eliminated and replaced by questions about classroom management in general. The variable of work involvement was added to the variable of deviancy. And preventing misbehavior was given higher investigative priority than handling misbehavior.

Accordingly, all classrooms were scored for work involvement and deviancy. Classroom management was defined as dealing with the surface behavior of children as measured by overt signs of work involvement and by deviancy. What is it that teachers do that correlates with these behaviors?

Some dimensions of teacher style were measured that correlated significantly with children's behavior in learning settings. These were:

1. *Withitness* and *overlapping*. These dimensions deal with a teacher's communicating that she knows what is going on regarding children's behavior and with her attending to

two issues simultaneously when two different issues are present.

2. *Smoothness* and *momentum*. These parameters measure how the teacher manages movement during recitations and at transition periods.

3. *Group alerting* and *accountability*. These aspects of a teacher's technique deal with the extent to which she maintains a group focus during recitations in contrast to becoming immersed in a single child.

4. *Valence* and *challenge arousal.*

5. *Seatwork variety* and *challenge*. This dimension deals with the teacher's programming learning activities with variety and intellectual challenge, especially in seatwork seetings.

The magnitude of the correlations between the above dimensions of teacher style and children's behavior depends upon whether one is dealing with the deviancy or work involvement of the children, or with recitation or seatwork as learning settings within the classroom.

It is possible, then, to delineate concrete aspects of teacher behavior that lead to managerial success in a classroom. These techniques of classroom management apply to emotionally disturbed children in regular classrooms as well as to nondisturbed children. They apply to boys as well as to girls. (We found no consistent differences between boys and girls in behavior scores, nor did we find that scores for managerial success correlated with the boy-girl ratios of the classrooms studied.) These techniques of classroom management apply to the group and not merely to individual children. They are techniques of creating an effective classroom ecology and learning milieu. One might note that none of them necessitate punitiveness or restrictiveness.

This focus upon group managerial techniques in classrooms is intended to go beyond simplified slogans such as "create rapport" or "make it interesting." Neither does this focus entail a preoccupation with such characteristics as "friendly," "warm," "patient," "understanding," "love for children," and similar attributes of people in general. These desirable attributes will not manage a classroom. Rather, the business of running a classroom is a complicated technology having to do with developing a nonsatiating learning program; programming for progress, challenge, and variety in learning activities; initiating and maintaining movement in classroom tasks with smoothness and momentum; coping with more than one event simultaneously; observing and emitting feedback for many different events; directing actions at appropriate targets; maintaining a focus upon a group; and doubtless other techniques not measured in these researches.

The mastery of classroom management skills should not be regarded as an end in itself. These techniques are, however, necessary tools. Techniques are enabling. The mastery of techniques enables one to do many different things. It makes choices possible. The possession of group management skills allows the teacher to accomplish her teaching goals—the absence of managerial skills acts as a barrier.

The focus upon group management skills is not opposed to a concern for individual children. The mastery of group management actually enables the teacher to program for individual differences and to help individual children. If there is a climate of work involvement and freedom from deviancy, different groups of children may be doing different things, and the teacher is free to help individual children if she so chooses.

One might say that a mastery of group management techniques enables a teacher to be free from concern about management.

REFERENCES

1. Alden, Elizabeth, 1960, The Effects on Non-Target Classmates of the Teacher's Use of Expert Power and Liking Power in Controlling Deviant Students. Doctoral dissertation, Wayne State University.
2. Barker, Roger C., and Herbert F. Wright, 1954, *Midwest and Its Children*. Evanston, Illinois: Row, Peterson & Company, Evanston, Ill. Page 532.
3. Biddle, B. J., 1954, An Application of Social Expectation Theory to the Initial Interview. Doctoral dissertation, University of Michigan.
4. Coburn, H. H., 1954, An Experimental Comparison of Relationship-Centered and Problem-Centered Counseling. Doctoral dissertation, Wayne State University.
5. Fenn, A. H., 1954, An Experimental Investigation of the Meanings of Understanding in the Counseling Relationship. Doctoral dissertation, Wayne State University.
6. Heider, Fritz, 1958, *The Psychology of Interpersonal Relations*. New York: John Wiley & Sons, Inc. Page 332.
7. Kounin, Jacob S., and Sylvia Obradovic, 1968, Managing Emotionally Disturbed Children in Regular Classrooms: A Replication and Extension. *J. special Educ.*, 2: 129–135.
8. Kounin, Jacob S., Wallace V. Friesen, and A. Evangeline Norton, 1966, Managing Emotionally Disturbed Children in Regular Classrooms. *J. educ. Psychol.*, 57: 1–13.
9. Kounin, Jacob S. and Paul V. Gump, 1961, The Comparative Influence of Punitive and Nonpunitive Teachers upon Children's Concepts of School Misconduct. *J. educ. Psychol.*, 52: 44–49.
10. Kounin, Jacob S., Paul V. Gump, and James J. Ryan, 111, 1961, Explorations in Classroom Management. *J. of Teacher Education*, 12: 235–247.
11. Kounin, Jacob S., N. Polansky, H. Coburn, and A. Fenn, 1956, Experimental Studies of Clients' Reactions to Initial Interviews. *Human Relations*, 9: 265–293.
12. Lewin, Kurt, 1935, *A Dynamic Theory of Personality: Selected Papers*. Translation, Donald K. Adams and Karl E. Zener. New York: McGraw-Hill, Inc. Page 286.
13. Ofchus, Leon T., 1960, Effects on Non-Target Classmates of Teachers' Efforts to Control Deviant Behavior. Doctoral dissertation, Wayne State University.
14. Osborn, Donald Keith, 1962, Saliencies in Students' Perceptions of Teachers. Doctoral dissertation, Wayne State University.
15. Polansky, Norman, and Jacob S. Kounin, 1956, Clients' Reactions to Initial Interviews. *Human Relations*, 9: 237–264.

Appendixes

Appendices

APPENDIX 1.1

**Distribution of Audience Reactions in Kindergarten to Incidents
of Low and High Desist Clarity**

	No Reaction	Disrup- tion	Con- formity	Noncon- formity	Ambiva- lence	Total
High clarity of desist	62 (63.5)[a]	31 (25.9)	24 (16.2)	13 (21)	10 (13.5)	140
Low clarity of desist	122 (120.5)	44 (49.1)	23 (30.8)	48 (40)	29 (25.5)	266
Totals	184	75	47	61	39	406

[a]All figures in parentheses are the theoretical frequencies.
$X^2 = 13.37 \ p < .01$

APPENDIX 1.2

**Distribution of Audience Reactions in Kindergarten to Desist Incidents
When Their Pre-Desist Orientations Were Deviant,
Deviancy Related, or Deviancy Free**

	No Reaction	Disrup- tion	Con- formity	Noncon- formity	Ambiva- lence	Total
Audience deviant	4 (20.8)[b]	3 (8.5)	12 (5.3)	11 (6.9)	16 (4.4)	46
Audience deviancy related	24 (33.6)	18 (13.7)	9 (8.6)	13 (11.1)	10 (7.1)	74
Audience deviancy free	156 (129.6)	54 (52.8)	26 (33.1)	37 (43)	13 (27.5)	286
Totals	184	75	47	61	39	406

[a]All figures in parentheses are the theoretical frequencies.
$X^2 = 77.76 \ p < .001$

APPENDIX 1.3

**Differences between the Content of Misconducts
and Consequences for Home, School, and Camp Milieus**

$(N = 170)$
H = Home; S = School; C = Camp

Content		p-Level
1. Targets		
Central adult	H > S > C	.001
(counseler, parent, teacher)		
Other kids	C > S > H	.001
2. Act Types		
Physical assaults	C > S > H	.01
Attack objects	H > S > C	.05
Noncompliance	H > S > C	.01
3. Objects of Suffering		
Central adult	H > S & C	.001
Other kids	C > S > H	.001
4. Retributors		
Central adult	S > H & C	.01
5. When There Is Retribution		
Personal punishment	H > S	.01
Reality interventions	S > H	.01
6. Content of Retributions		
Physical punishment	H > C > S	.001
Ego-loss	S > H & C	.001

APPENDIX 1.4

**Differences between the Dimensions of Misconducts
and Consequences for Home, School, and Camp Milieus**

$$(N = 170)$$
H = Home; S = School; C = Camp

Dimensions		*p-Level*
1. Gross milieu likelihood	C = Improbable	
	S = Moderate	
	H = High likely	.001
2. Milieu seriousness	C & H = Trivial	
	S = Moderate	.001
3. Coder seriousness	C & H = Trivial	
	S = Moderate	.02
4. Intention of the perpetrator	C = Premeditated	
	H = Accidental	
	S = Intentional	.001
5. Ego-acceptability	C = Ego-alien	
	H = "Accidents"	
	S = Ego-acceptable	.001
6. Consequence likelihood	C = Unlikely	
	S = High likely	.05
7. Seriousness of consequence to others	C = Serious	
	S & H = Not serious	.02
8. Seriousness of retribution to perpetrator	C = Low	
	S = Medium	
	H = High	.01
9. Destructiveness	H & C > S	.001
10. Destructive impulses toward objects	H > C & S	.01
11. Destructive impulses toward people	C > H & S	.01

APPENDIX 2.1

High School Interview Schedule*

Name	*Date*
Sex	*Period*
School	*Interviewer*

Introduction:

      I'm   from Wayne State University. We're trying to learn more about how to run classrooms so that we'll know how to make schools better. We feel that we can learn about this by finding out what students like yourself think about how classrooms should be run. Now we're not checking up on anybody — you, any of the teachers (in fact, we don't even know any of them), any school, or anybody. Anything you say will be just between you and me. So you'll help us most by telling us frankly as possible what you think about how classes you know are run. Okay?

I. a. What academic subjects are you taking now?

    1.   3.

    2.   4.

   b. You know, in some classes you go in determined to learn and in others you may not care so much. Now when you go into classes in these subjects, how determined are you to learn? Let's take . . . (1st one mentioned in 1.a., 2nd, etc.; label each).

I don't care about learning	I am somewhat determined to learn	I am very determined to learn
.	.	.

   c. How determined are the other kids to learn? Let's take the kids in . . . (name Hi-M class). Now the kids in . . . (name Lo-M class).

    *Hi-M class refers to the class for which the student stated that highest degree of motivation to learn. Lo-M refers to the class with the student's lowest degree of motivation to learn. This interview was conducted separately for each student for both Hi-M and Lo-M classes.

They don't care about learning	They are somewhat determined to learn	They are very determined to learn
.	.	.

d. In general, how much do you feel like fooling around in _____?
(Hi-M); in _____? (Lo-M). (Label.)

Practically always	Medium	Practically never
.	.	.

Why (difference)?

e. In general, how much do the other kids fool around in _____
(Hi-M); in _____ (Lo-M)? (Label.)

Practically always	Medium	Practically never
.	.	.

Why (difference)?

II. We're interested in finding out what goes on in a class when someone misbehaves. You know that even in the best class somebody misbehaves at some time or another. This misbehavior may be very serious or very minor. The teacher may have just snapped her finger, maybe just looked at the student who misbehaved, or reprimanded or punished the student in some way.

   a. Now think of the last time—which you remember clearly—that the teacher in _____ (Hi-M) tried to stop some misbehavior in class. (Pause.) Start by telling me where you were and what you were doing just before it happened. Then, what did the student do, what did the teacher do and say?

   To Interviewer: Above description should enable the reader to visualize the T-D drama. Physical position; T's locomotion (if any), gestures, posture, facial expression, tone of voice and words.

   b. What did the student do after the teacher did that? (Conform eagerly, grudgingly, defiantly—or not conform.)

c. Why do you suppose the teacher interfered—did something about it?

d. The teacher could have done different things. Why do you suppose she (he) handled it the WAY she (he) did?

e. What do you think about how it was handled?

f. How did the WHOLE event affect you?

g. How did the event change your ideas about the teacher?

h. (If no change in g.) Well, you know sometimes we don't *change* our ideas about someone but we become *more* or *less* sure of what we already thought. In what way did it make you more or less sure about what you already thought about the teacher?

i. How much attention were you paying to the subject just before it happened?

None at all	Medium amount	As much as possible
.	.	.

j. (In case of less than ¾'s attention) What were you occupied with? (e.g., daydream, watching others, talking, watching deviancy.)

k. (Forced-choice)

    1. Was student involved boy   or girl   ?

    2. How well did you know the student(s) who did it?
    __Knew very well *and* __Liked well __Liked some __Disliked
    __Knew fairly well *and* __Liked   __"So-So"   __Disliked
    __Didn't know
    (If student *known*, ask:) How did what happened affect your ideas about him (her)?
    (If student *not* known, ask:) What notions or impressions about him (her) did you get from what happened?

    3. How wrong was what the student did?

Not wrong at all	Somewhat wrong	Very wrong
.	.	.

4. (Interviewer, check *one* of these blanks)
Was what the kid did an accident?__ (If no, ask:) Did he do it to cause trouble or bait the teacher__or did he just do it __?

5. Considering what the kid did, did you feel the T made too little or too much of an issue of it?

Way too little	Somewhat too little	About right	A little too much	Way too much
.		.		.

6. Was there any humor in how T handled it? Very much _____
Some _____
None _____
(If humor is checked and not apparent to you by description, ask:)
How was it humorous?

7. How determined was the teacher to stop what was going on?
____Extremely determined; nothing was going to stop her (him)
____Pretty determined
____Sort of determined, not too concerned
____Not at all determined, as if *really* didn't care

8. Was T: _____Very angry
_____Pretty angry
_____Somewhat irritated or irked
_____Calm, no irritation at all

9. How fairly was it handled?

Extremely unfair	Not particularly fair or unfair	Extremely fair
.	.	.

10. Compare how much attention you paid to the subject after this happened as to attention before it happened.

Paid very much LESS attention to subject	About same	Paid very much MORE attention to subject
.	.	.

11. Did you *feel* like acting good yourself after it happened?

| No, I wanted | I wanted | I really wanted |
| to misbehave | to behave some | to behave good |

     .   .   .

12. (If answer on 11 indicates conformity, ask:) However, did you perhaps also feel like misbehaving yourself in some way after it happened?

| No | Just a little | Yes, I felt |
| | | like misbehaving |

.   .   .

(If any tendency to misbehave is offered in 11 or 12 ask: What did you do?)

13. Sometimes these things affect our feelings a bit. Did you feel uneasy or uncomfortable or perhaps a little embarrassed by what happened?

_____Yes, a lot   _____Some   _____No

(If "yes" or "some," underline which feeling and probe for why feeling arose.)

14. Were you inclined to take teacher's or student's side?

| Very much on | Neither | Very much on |
| student's side | | teacher's side |

     .   .   .

III. a. How does this teacher (Hi-M) generally keep students from misbehaving in class?

b. Was what happened this time any surprise to you?   _____No
_____A little
_____ Yes,
a lot

(If not, No.)
_____Surprised only by what the kid did
_____Surprised only by the way the teacher handled it
_____Surprised both by what the kid did and by the way T handled it.

Why surprised?

IV. You know, some of a teacher's efforts are devoted to teaching and explaining the subject and some to keeping order and controlling behavior. Compared to most teachers, how much effort does this teacher give to keeping order?

No time spent in keeping order	Some time spent in keeping order	A lot of time spent in keeping order	Practically ALL time spent in keeping order
.	.	.	.

V. Suppose a friend of yours was trying to decide whether to get this T (Hi-M) for (subject) or not. What would you tell him (her) about T? How would you describe T? (Probe for answers with vague meanings: "tough," "good," to see if concepts refer to PERSONAL, CONTROL, or TASK areas.)

VI. (Forced-choice) [Use same sheet for Hi-M class (red) and Lo-M class (pencil) and probe for differences over 2 inches.]

Introduction: We realize you've only been in classes a few times and are not sure about some things. But just give us how it seems to you up to now.

1. Judging from what's happened so far, how much do you expect to learn in class _____ (Hi-M or Lo-M)? Compare with other classes you're taking.

Very much less than any	Average	Very much more than any
.	.	.

Why the difference?

2. How much have you learned in class _____? Compare with your other classes.

Very much less than any	Average	Very much more than any
.	.	.

3. How much are you interested in class work in class _____ (Hi-M or Lo-M)?

Very much less than any	Average	Very much more than any
.	.	.

Why the difference?
How well do you generally behave in this class?

Extremely bad	Neither good nor bad	Extremely good
.	.	.

Why?

5. How much do you like the teacher?

Dislike very much	Neither like nor dislike	Like extremely well
.	.	.

Why?

6. You know, there are teachers you like to talk to about your questions or ideas in (Hi-M—Lo-M). Others you wouldn't care to talk to. How much would you like to talk to the teacher—about some question or idea in (Hi-M—Lo-M)?

Be the LAST T I'd talk to	Neither like to talk to nor dislike to talk to	Be the FIRST T I'd talk to
.	.	.

Why?

7. How much would you like to talk to your (Hi-M—Lo-M) teacher about some personal problem?

Be the LAST T I'd talk to	Neither like to talk to nor dislike to talk to	Be the FIRST T I'd talk to
.	.	.

Why?

8. How much do you think the teacher knows about the subject?

Hardly anything. Not enough for this course	Just enough for this course	Everything. More than enough to teach any class
.	.	.

Why?

9. How well is this teacher able to handle a class?

Terrible. Couldn't handle a class at all	Neither good nor bad	Best possible. Can handle a class very well
.	.	.

Why? (Reasons why Lo is Lo and Hi is Hi.)

10. Some classes seem "together" with the teacher and the class activity; others are not. How together would you say (Hi-M or Lo-M) is?

Not at all w/T & class activity	Somewhat w/T & class activity	Very much w/T & class activity
.	.	.

11. (If below middle on 10)
Sometimes you may get the feeling that the class is banded together against the teacher. Is that true in (Hi-M or Lo-M)?

All split up, no togetherness	Somewhat together & against the T	All together & against the T
.	.	.

APPENDIX 2.2

**The Frequency with Which Students Use the Following Bases
When Evaluating Teachers' Methods of Handling Misbehavior**

Basis for Evaluation (approval or disapproval)	*High Motivation To Learn Classes*		*Low Motivation To Learn Classes*		*Total Number*	*Total Percent*
	Number	Percent	Number	Percent		
No reason given	81	64.8	74	59.2	155	62.0
Equity	12	9.6	19	15.2	31	12.4
Effectiveness	20	16.0	7	5.6	27	10.8
Intensity appropriateness	6	4.8	20	16.0	26	10.4
Miscellaneous	6	4.8	5	4.0	11	4.4
Totals	125	100.0	125	100.0	250	100.0

APPENDIX 2.3

**Frequency and Percent of Reasons
Attributed to Teachers for Interfering with the Deviancy**

Attributed Reason for Interfering	*High Motivation To Learn Classes*		*Low Motivation To Learn Classes*		*Total Number*	*Total Percent*
	Number	Percent	Number	Percent		
Restore or maintain learning conditions	63	50.4	60	48.0	123	49.2
Justice and equity	24	19.2	18	14.4	42	16.8
Express teacher's feelings	12	9.6	24	19.2	36	14.4
Ambiguous answers	18	14.4	17	13.6	35	14.0
Authority	6	4.8	4	3.2	10	4.0
Others	2	1.6	2	1.6	4	1.6
Totals	125	100.0	125	100.0	250	100.0

APPENDIX 2.4

**Frequency and Percent of Reasons Attributed to Teachers
for Managing the Deviancy in the Manner Reported**

Attributed Reason for Teacher's Choice of Desist Technique	High Motivation To Learn Classes		Low Motivation To Learn Classes		Total Number	Total Percent
	Number	Percent	Number	Percent		
Limit severity	59	47.2	30	24.0	89	35.6
Express teacher's feeling	18	14.4	30	24.0	48	19.2
Ambiguous answers	19	15.2	27	21.6	46	18.4
Task facilitating	7	5.6	8	6.4	15	6.0
Punitive	5	4.0	10	8.0	15	6.0
Authority	6	4.8	8	6.4	14	5.6
Benevolent	5	4.0	1	.8	6	2.4
Deviant as example	2	1.6	4	3.2	6	2.4
Good way	3	2.4	2	1.6	5	2.0
Justice and equity	1	.8	3	2.4	4	1.6
No response	0	0.0	2	1.6	2	.8
Totals	125	100.0	125	100.0	250	100.0

APPENDIX 2.5

**Differences between Students' Reactions to Desist Events
in Classes with High and Low Motivation to Learn**

Kind of Impact	[a]N	p-Level of Difference	Direction of Difference
A. *Audience Behavior Reactions*			
1. Conformity-deviancy	250	.01	High more conformity inclination; Low more deviancy inclination
2. Attention to task prior to desist	250	.01	High more attention
3. Change in attention after desist	240	.10	High more increase; Low more decrease
4. Discomfort	250	NS	
B. *Judgments about the Desist Event*			
1. Side with teacher or deviant	250	.01	High side more with teacher
2. Fairness	249	.001	High more fair
3. Appropriateness of teacher's reaction	241	.05	High more appropriate; Low more excessive teacher reaction
4. Approval-disapproval	240	.01	High more approval
C. *Judgments about Deviancy*			
1. Intrusiveness of deviancy	250	.05	High more judged intrusiveness
2. Seriousness of deviancy	250	NS	
D. *Perceptions of Desist*			
1. Punishment only	250	.05	Low described more pure punishment
2. Rated anger	248	.001	Low rated more teacher anger
3. Described clarity	245	.001	High described more teacher deviancy-cessation information
4. Harm to deviant	250	.10	

APPENDIX 2.5 (cont.)

Kind of Impact	[a]N	p-Level of Difference	Direction of Difference
E. *Attributed Reasons for Teacher Desisting*			
1. Reasons for interfering	190	.10	High tend to give more restoration of learning; Low more reaction
2. Reasons for choice of desist	246	.01	Low more reaction; High more severity limitation
3. Reasons for approval of desist	95	.01	High more effectiveness; Low more equity

[a] *N*'s are not always 250 since the answers to some questions were not always codeable, or were coded as "vacuous" or "no answer."

APPENDIX 2.6

Differences between High Motivation (N = 125) and Low Motivation Classes Determined Separately for Low Motivation Plus Teacher Liked Classes (N = 68) and Low Motivation Plus Teacher Disliked Classes (N = 57)

Kind of Impact	p-Level of Difference between High Motivation and Low Motivation Plus Liked Teachers	Difference in Favor of	p-Level of Difference between High Motivation and Low Motivation Plus Disliked Teachers	Difference in Favor of
Task attention	.01	High Motivation	.01	High Motivation
Task attention change	.10	High Motivation	.10	High Motivation
Behavior conformity	.01	High Motivation	.01	High Motivation
Fairness	NS		.001	High Liking
Support of teacher	NS		.001	High Liking
Teacher overreaction	NS		.001	Low Liking
Described anger of desist	NS		.05	Low Liking
Rated anger of desist	NS		.001	Low Liking
Firmness of desist	NS		.02	Low Liking
Harm to deviant	NS		.01	Low Liking
Intrusiveness of deviancy	.05	High Motivation	.05	High Motivation
Seriousness of deviancy	NS		NS	

APPENDIX 2.7

**Percentage of Students Mentioning a Teacher Attribute
for High Motivation and Low Motivation Classes
and for High Liked and Low Liked Teachers**

(Number of Mentions = 933)

Category	High Motivation[a]		Low Motivation[a]	
	High Liked $N = 105$ Percent	Low Liked $N = 18$ Percent	High Liked $N = 67$ Percent	Low Liked $N = 56$ Percent
Personal Attributes				
1. Friendly, understanding	6.77	3.51	9.63	.61
2. Harsh, grouchy	.52	10.52	1.67	12.20
3. Humor	1.30	0.00	1.67	2.44
4. Deviate teacher	1.04	1.75	1.26	6.71
5. Neutral teacher	.78	0.00	1.67	3.04
6. Like teacher	12.49	3.51	16.32	1.21
7. Dislike teacher	.26	7.02	1.26	10.98
Total % Personal Attributes:				
Interview I	23.17	26.33	33.47	37.20
Interview II	23.04	25.23	24.26	22.00
Managerial Attributes				
8. High tolerance	9.11	8.77	5.86	3.66
9. Low tolerance	3.91	14.03	5.02	18.29
10. Justice	5.73	5.26	2.93	.61
Total % Managerial Attributes:				
Interview I	18.75	28.06	13.81	22.56
Interview II	14.61	19.99	15.95	18.50
Task Attributes				
11. Explains well	11.19	8.77	7.95	2.44
12. Explains poorly	.26	0.00	.84	6.10
13. Knowledge subject matter (+)	2.34	3.51	2.51	1.21

14. Knowledge subject matter (−)	.26	0.00	0.00	.61
15. Task Approach (+)	15.88	15.79	12.97	2.44
16. Task approach (−)	1.04	3.51	1.67	9.15
17. Work demands (Great)	6.77	1.75	7.53	7.32
18. Work demands (Few)	4.69	5.26	6.28	2.44
19. Evaluation of demand (+)	4.95	0.00	4.60	1.21
20. Evaluation of demand (−)	.78	.41	3.35	4.27
21. Task interesting	9.64	8.77	5.02	1.83
22. Task not interesting	.26	0.00	0.00	1.21
Total % Task Attributes:				
Interview I	58.08	45.61	52.72	40.24
Interview II	62.35	54.70	58.79	59.50

[a]The *N*'s do not correspond to the total *N*'s because a few descriptions were too meager to code, such as: "He's O.K., I guess."

APPENDIX 3.1

**A Comparison of Attitudes toward School Misconducts
Held by Children with Punitive and Nonpunitive First Grade Teachers**[a]

Misconducts and Explanations	*% of Punitive N = 84*	*% of Non-punitive N = 90*
I. Content and quality of the misconducts		
A. Physical assaults on others	38	17
B. Milieu-serious misconducts	89	63
C. Coder-serious misconducts	48	27
D. Abstract misconducts	27	52
II. Content and quality of the explanations		
A. Peers as objects of consequences	94	61
B. Physical damage to objects of consequences	60	23
C. Serious harm to others	45	18
D. Reality-centered retributions	21	48
E. "Reflexive justifications" as explanations	11	26
III. Role of self in misconducts		
A. Ego-alien misconducts	26	11
B. Premeditated misconducts	29	15
IV. Aggression		
A. Overall aggression ("blood and guts")	49	24
V. Concern with school-unique objectives		
A. Learning and achievement losses	20	43
B. Institutional law violations	49	62

[a]All differences in percentages in this table are significant at the .05 level or below.

APPENDIX 4.1

**Correlations between Teacher Style and Children's
Behavior in Recitation and Seatwork Settings[a]**

$N = 49$ classrooms (r of .276 significant at .05 level)

	Recitation		Seatwork	
	Work Involve- ment	Freedom from Deviancy	Work Involve- ment	Freedom from Deviancy
Momentum (Freedom from Slowdowns)[b]	.656	.641	.198	.490
Withitness	.615	.531	.307	.509
Smoothness (Freedom from Thrusts, Dangles, Stimulus-Boundedness)	.601	.489	.382	.421
Group Alerting	.603	.442	.234	.290
Accountability	.494	.385	.002	−.035
Overlappingness	.460	.362	.259	.379
Valence and Challenge Arousal	.372	.325	.308	.371
Seatwork Variety and Challenge	.061	.033	.516	.276
Recitation Variety and Challenge	.238	.162		
Overall Variety and Challenge	.217	.099	.449	.194
Average Duration of Seatwork Activities ("Attention Span")			.231	.005
Class Size (Range 21–39)	−.279	−.258	−.152	−.249
Boy-Girl Ratio	−.132	−.097	−.197	−.171
Maximum Multiple R's	.812	.720	.686	.741

[a]Goodness of fit tests for the various measures of teacher style and for the measures of children's behavior showed that the distributions of scores did not differ significantly from a normal distribution curve.

[b]Intercoder agreements for the various measures of children's behavior and teacher styles ranged from 79% to 99% agreement, with an average intercoder agreement of 92%.

APPENDIX 4.2

Intercorrelations among Teacher Style Measures

	Momentum	Withit-ness	Smooth-ness	Group Alert-ing	Account-ability	Overlap-ping	Valence and Challenge Arousal	Seatwork Variety and Challenge	Class Size
Momentum		.499	.745	.294	.385	.404	.268	−.091	−.160
Withitness			.479	.474	.370	.598	.271	.224	−.097
Smoothness				.420	.289	.482	.259	−.037	−.069
Group Alerting					.494	.416	.347	.080	−.145
Accountability						.275	.161	.084	−.076
Overlapping							.067	.039	−.136
Valence and Challenge Arousal								.325	−.084
Seatwork Variety and Challenge									−.206
Class Size									

APPENDIX 4.3

Correlations and First Order Partial Correlations between Teacher Style and Work Involvement in Recitation Settings

	Momentum	Withit-ness	Group Alert-ing	Smooth-ness	Account-ability	Overlap-ping	Valence and Challenge Arousal	Seatwork Variety and Challenge	Class Size
Pearson r	.656	.615	.603	.601	.494	.460	.372	.061	−.279
Variable held constant:									
Momentum		.439	.569	.222	.347	.283	.270	.161	−.234
Withitness	.511		.449	.442	.364	.146	.270	−.099	−.280
Group Alerting	.628	.468		.480	.283	.288	.217	.016	−.243
Smoothness	.391	.466	.484		.418	.243	.281	.105	−.299
Accountability	.581	.535	.475	.550		.388	.341	.023	−.279
Overlapping	.599	.477	.510	.487	.430		.385	.049	−.246
Valence and Challenge Arousal	.622	.575	.545	.563	.474	.470		−.068	−.268
Seatwork Variety and Challenge	.666	.618	.602	.604	.492	.459	.373		−.273
Class Size	.645	.615	.592	.607	.494	.444	.364	.004	

APPENDIX 4.4

Correlations and First Order Partial Correlations between Teacher Style and Freedom from Deviancy in Recitation Settings

	Momentum	Withit-ness	Smooth-ness	Group Alert-ing	Account-ability	Overlap-ping	Valence and Challenge Arousal	Seatwork Variety and Challenge	Class Size
Pearson r	.641	.531	.489	.442	.385	.361	.325	.033	−.258
Variable held constant:									
Momentum		.318	.022	.345	.195	.146	.208	.120	−.205
Withitness	.512		.315	.254	.239	.065	.222	−.104	−.245
Smoothness	.476	.388		.298	.291	.165	.236	.059	−.258
Group Alerting	.596	.408	.373		.213	.218	.204	−.003	−.219
Accountability	.579	.454	.427	.313		.288	.289	.001	−.249
Overlapping	.580	.422	.385	.343	.318		.324	.020	−.226
Valence and Challenge Arousal	.608	.487	.443	.371	.356	.360		−.081	−.245
Seatwork Variety and Challenge	.647	.538	.491	.441	.383	.361	.333		−.257
Class Size	.629	.528	.489	.423	.379	.341	.315	−.021	

APPENDIX 4.5

Correlations and First Order Partial Correlations between Teacher Style and Work Involvement in Seatwork Settings

	Seatwork Variety and Challenge	Smooth- ness	Valence and Challenge Arousal	Withit- ness	Overlap- ping	Group Alert- ing	Momentum	Account- ability	Class Size
Pearson r	.516	.382	.308	.307	.259	.234	.198	.002	−.152
Variable held constant:									
Seatwork Variety and Challenge		.468	.173	.230	.279	.225	.288	−.046	−.054
Smoothness	.574		.234	.153	.093	.088	−.139	−.122	−.136
Valence and Challenge Arousal	.462	.329		.244	.252	.142	.127	−.050	−.133
Withitness	.482	.281	.245		.099	.105	.055	−.126	−.129
Overlapping	.524	.303	.302	.196		.143	.106	−.074	−.122
Group Alerting	.513	.321	.249	.229	.183		.139	−.134	−.122
Momentum	.547	.358	.270	.245	.120	.187		−.082	−.124
Accountability	.517	.398	.312	.329	.269	.268	.214		−.152
Class Size	.501	.377	.300	.297	.244	.217	.178	−.009	

APPENDIX 4.6

Correlations and First Order Partial Correlations between Teacher Style and Freedom from Deviancy in Seatwork Settings

	Withit-ness	Momentum	Smooth-ness	Overlap-ping	Valence and Challenge Arousal	Group Alert-ing	Seatwork Variety and Challenge	Account-ability	Class Size
Pearson r	.509	.490	.421	.379	.371	.289	.276	−.035	−.249
Variable held constant:									
Withitness		.316	.234	.107	.281	.064	.193	−.278	−.234
Momentum	.350		.096	.228	.286	.174	.370	−.277	−.199
Smoothness	.386	.291		.222	.299	.137	.322	−.180	−.244
Overlapping	.380	.398	.293		.375	.157	.282	−.156	−.216
Valence and Challenge Arousal	.457	.437	.362	.383		.185	.177	−.103	−.236
Group Alerting	.441	.442	.344	.297	.301		.265	−.214	−.219
Seatwork Variety and Challenge	.477	.538	.449	.383	.310	.279		−.060	−.205
Accountability	.562	.545	.450	.405	.382	.353	.280		−.253
Class Size	.503	.471	.418	.360	.363	.264	.237	−.056	

Index

A

Accountability, and correlations with children's behavior, 123

meaning and measurement of, 119–122

and relation to group alerting, 123–124

Alden, Elizabeth, 51, 55, 58, 145

Attention span, 128

B

Barker, Roger C., 60, 145

Biddle, Bruce J., 51, 145, 146

C

Camp, concepts of misconduct in, 17–18, 141–142

and differences from school, 17–19, 141

ripple effects of desist at, 13–15, 141

Coburn, H. H., 51, 145, 146

Commitment, effect on ripple effect, 34–40

D

Dangles, 100–101

Desists, definition of, 2

and anger and punitiveness, 9, 27, 28, 38, 54–55, 168

child treatment within, 68–69

and clarity, 9, 28, 65

differences between experiments and field studies, 55–57, 142–143

differences between first day and later days, 12

forms of, 68

and humor, 28

and harm, 28

intensity of, 49, 67

and firmness, 9, 28, 38, 66

Desists (*continued*)
  perceived reasons for, 26, 161, 162
  and results of videotape study, 64–74
  supportive, 5–6
  threatening, 5–6
Discipline (*see* Desists)

E

Emotionally disturbed children, and contagion of misbehavior, 64, 75
  effects of teachers upon, 63, 75
  and relation of behavior to behavior of nondisturbed, 75
  selection of, 60, 63
Experiments, college, 1–7
  contrast with field studies, 49–51, 55–57, 71–73, 142–143
  high school, 47–52

F

Fenn, A. H., 51, 146
Flip-flops, 101
Format, and correlations with children's behavior, 122
  meaning and measurement of, 115–117
Fragmentation, group, 105–106
  prop or actone, 106
Friesen, Wallace V., 60, 146

G

Group alerting, and correlations with children's behavior, 122–123
  meaning and scoring of, 117–119
  and relation with accountability, 123–124

Group focus, general meaning and examples, 109–113
  scoring of, 113–115, 121–122
  See also Group alerting; Format; Accountability
Gump, Paul V., 2, 47, 146

H

Heider, Fritz, 37, 146
High school, experiment on ripple effect in, 22–55
  and interview schedule, 152–162
  kinds of desists in, 24
  kinds of misbehavior in, 23
  kinds of ripple effects in, 25–27
  study of desists and ripple effects in, 22–55
Home, concepts of misconduct in, 18–21

J

Jerkiness (*see* Smoothness)

K

Kindergarten, ripple effects of desists in, 7–12
Kounin, Jacob S., 46, 47, 51, 63, 145, 146

L

Lewin, Kurt, 126, 146
Liking for teacher, balance theory in, 37–40
  and effect on ripple effect, 31–34, 42–43, 51, 165
  factors associated with, 43–47
  and relation to motivation to learn, 31–32

M

Milieu effects, in concepts of misconduct, 15–22, 150–151
in perception of central adults, 20–21, 46–47, 141
in ripple effect, 14–15, 48–51, 57–59, 141–143
Misbehavior, at camp, 17–18
in high school, 23
at home, 18–19
in school, 17–21
See also Superego
Momentum (*see* Slowdowns)
Motivation to learn, effects on ripple effect, 29–31, 40–41, 50–51, 163–164
factors associated with, 43–46
and relation to liking for teacher, 31–32, 42–43
Movement management, 92–97
See also Smoothness; Slowdowns

N

Norton, A. Evangeline, 60, 146

O

Observation, advantages of videotape, 63
and inadequacies of human observers, 60–63
requirements of, 62
Obradovich, Sylvia, 63, 146
Ofchus, Leon T., 23, 146
Osborne, Donald Keith, 44, 51, 146
Overdwelling, actone, 103
behavior, 102
prop, 103–104
task, 104–105
Overlapping, meaning of, 84–86
and relation to child behavior, 88, 169

Overlapping (*continued*)
and relation to withitness, 88–91
scoring of, 87

P

Polansky, Norman, 46, 51, 146

R

Ripple effects, definition of, 2
camp study of, 13–15
and college experiment, 2–7
and threatening desist, 5–6
and supportive desist, 5–6
effect of audience orientation on, 11–12, 149
effect of length of time in school on, 12
effect of motivation to learn on, 29–31, 40–41
high school study of, 22–55
kindergarten study of, 7–12
and clarity, 9–11, 149
and firmness, 9–11
and anger and punitiveness, 9–11
Ryan, James J. III, 2, 47, 146

S

Satiation, definition of, 126–127
and correlation of variety with children's behavior, 136–139, 169
and differences between early and later elementary grades, 75, 137
measurement of, 127–136
progress cues of, 128–130
and valence and challenge arousal 130–131
and variety, 131–138
Slowdowns, examples of, 95–97, 102–107

Slowdowns (*continued*)
  and fragmentation, 105–107
  measurement of, 106
  and overdwelling, 102–105
  and relation to children's be-
    havior, 107, 169
  and relation to smoothness,
    107–108
Smoothness, and dangles,
    100–101
  examples of, 93–95, 98–101
  and flip-flops, 101
  measurement of, 101–102
  and relation to children's be-
    havior, 107, 169
  and relation to momentum,
    107–108
  and stimulus-boundedness, 98
  and thrusts, 100
  and truncations, 101
Stevenson, Burton, 146
Stimulus-boundedness, 98
Superego, and camp and school,
    contrast between, 17–18
  and home and school, contrast
    between, 18–21
  study of, 15–21
  See also Misbehavior

T

Teachers, and contrast with other
    professionals, 46–47
  saliencies in perception of,
    43–47, 166–167
  See also Liking for teachers
Thrusts, 100
Truncations, 101

V

Variety (*see* Satiation)
Videotape studies, major, 74–139
  and measurement of child
    behavior, 63–64, 76–79

Videotape studies (*continued*)
  preliminary, 62–74
  and scoring of teacher behavi-
    or, 79
  selection of classrooms for, 63,
    76
  technique of, 63

W

Withitness, meaning of, 73–85
  scoring of, 82–85
  and relation to overlapping,
    88–91
  and relation to child behavior,
    88, 169
Wright, Herbert F., 60, 145

DATE DUE
REMINDER

MAY 2 0 2005

~~NOV 10 2009~~

NOV 1 0 2009

Please do not remove
this date due slip.